Costs and Outcomes in Children's Social Care

of related interest

Fostering Now
Messages from Research
Ian Sinclair
Foreword by Tom Jeffreys, Director General, Children, Young People and Families Directorate, DfES
ISBN 1 84310 362 1

Foster Children
Where They Go and How They Get On
Ian Sinclair, Claire Baker, Kate Wilson and Ian Gibbs
ISBN 1 84310 278 1

Foster Carers
Why They Stay and Why They Leave
Ian Sinclair, Ian Gibbs and Kate Wilson
ISBN 1 84310 172 6

Foster Placements
Why They Succeed and Why They Fail
Ian Sinclair, Kate Wilson and Ian Gibbs
ISBN 1 84310 173 4

Supporting Parents
Messages from Research
David Quinton
Foreword by the Right Honourable Margaret Hodge, Minister for Children, Young People and Families
ISBN 1 84310 210 2

Family Support as Reflective Practice
Edited by Pat Dolan, John Canavan and John Pinkerton
Foreword by Neil Thompson
ISBN 1 84310 320 6

Enhancing the Well-being of Children and Families through Effective Interventions
International Evidence for Practice
Edited by Colette McAuley, Peter J. Pecora and Wendy Rose
Foreword by Maria Eagle MP
ISBN 1 84310 116 5

The Developing World of the Child
Edited by Jane Aldgate, David Jones, Wendy Rose and Carole Jeffery
Foreword by Maria Eagle MP
ISBN 1 84310 244 7

Safeguarding and Promoting the Well-being of Children, Families and Communities
Edited by Jane Scott and Harriet Ward
Foreword by Maria Eagle MP
ISBN 1 84310 141 6

Babies and Young Children in Care
Life Pathways, Decision-making and Practice
Harriet Ward, Emily R. Munro and Chris Dearden
ISBN 1 84310 272 2

Costs and Outcomes in Children's Social Care

Messages from Research

Jennifer Beecham and Ian Sinclair

Foreword by Parmjit Dhanda MP

Jessica Kingsley Publishers
London and Philadelphia

First published in 2007
by Jessica Kingsley Publishers
116 Pentonville Road
London N1 9JB, UK
and
400 Market Street, Suite 400
Philadelphia, PA 19106, USA

www.jkp.com

Library of Congress Cataloging in Publication Data

Beecham, Jennifer.
Costs and outcomes in children's social care : messages from research / Jennifer Beecham and Ian Sinclair ; foreword by Parmjit Dhanda. -- 1st paperback ed.
p. cm. -- (Costs and effectiveness of services for children in need)
Includes bibliographical references and index.
ISBN-13: 978-1-84310-496-4 (pbk. : alk. paper)
ISBN-10: 1-84310-496-2 (pbk. : alk. paper) 1. Children--Services for--Great Britain. 2. Social service--Great Britain--Costs. I. Sinclair, Ian, 1938- II. Title.
HV245.B44 2007
362.70941--dc22

2006027891

British Library Cataloguing in Publication Data
A CIP catalogue record for this book is available from the British Library

ISBN-13: 978 1 84310 496 4
ISBN-10: 1 84310 496 2

Printed and bound in the United Kingdom by The Alden Group, Oxford

Contents

List of Tables, Figures and Boxes

Foreword

In the years since the Government took office there has been a major policy focus on the quality and organisation of support for children and families. In Every Child Matters we set out a programme of radical reforms to the services for children and young people. And we have always been clear that these reforms should be for the benefit of all. The gap must be closed between the achievement of the most fortunate and those who face the greatest obstacles to achieving their potential. Our most important objective of all is getting better outcomes for the most vulnerable children and young people in our society.

Good planning and commissioning is at the heart of improving outcomes for children and young people. Every local area both plans and commissions children's services. No single agency can deliver any one of the five outcomes for children. This is why we have set in place arrangements for joint commissioning and pooled budgets. Local partners work will need to work together to set priorities for action, identify and pool relevant resources, plan services and decide how best to purchase or provide them.

To plan effectively we need a sound understanding of how the money is currently spent and the impact on children and families. We need to know how resources are distributed between different services at the moment and why they are distributed in this way, and what changes are practical. We need to know what services are effective. And we need to know more about why costs appear to differ dramatically from one authority to another.

From the beginning the Government's commitment to improve services has included a firm understanding that changes had to be based on sound evidence. That's why six years ago we funded a major research programme to find out more about the relationship between cost and outcomes in children's services.

The research in the Costs and Effectiveness of Services to Children in Need initiative, which is summarised in this book, amply demonstrates the need for reform as well as the part that research can play in providing the tools for change. Studies in this initiative are among the first to estimate unit costs for children's social care services and social work processes, and to calculate the costs of care packages that cross usual service and agency boundaries. The studies cover a diverse range of topics from supporting families with young children in their own homes to looking at staff motivations and skills in services for children looked after by local authorities.

This is an excellent and timely summary of a highly relevant group of studies and I commend it to all those who plan and deliver children's services.

Parmjit Dhanda MP
Parliamentary Under Secretary of State for Children, Young People and Families

Acknowledgements

This overview can only deal with a fraction of the work undertaken by those whose studies are reported. We thank the researchers who have willingly given their time and expertise to draft summaries of their research and comment on the book itself. Obviously the final responsibility for the selection and interpretation of the material lies with us as authors.

Like the researchers we are also extremely grateful to all the young people, staff and other participants who made the original studies possible. Their willingness to contribute their hard won experience in the hope of benefiting others is impressive. We owe a further debt to those young people and their families and carers who contributed more directly to the work of the Implementation and Advisory Group.

As authors we have been admirably supported by the Implementation and Advisory Group itself. Its members have worked far beyond the call of duty in reading the research reports, identifying themes and perspectives, and in providing invaluable observations on the numerous drafts. Particular thanks are due to Celia Atherton who organised and led the Group with singular energy, good humour and tact.

Finally we owe a particular debt to Carolyn Davies, the Group's chair. Without her commitment to child social care research – in both outcomes and costs – this overview would not have existed.

Jennifer Beecham and Ian Sinclair

Chapter 1

Introducing the Book

Introduction

Care services for children depend on a limited supply of resources; it is vital that these are used to best effect. Against this background, and in a context of concern about rising costs, the Department of Health (DoH) commissioned a programme of research on the Costs and Effectiveness of Services for Children in Need. Following a transfer of responsibilities, the Department for Education and Skills (DfES) has taken forward this initiative and supported the overview of its findings. This book is the result. It summarises the findings from this research programme, pulling out some core policy and practice themes.

As the title implies, these findings are about the way services are delivered, the costs of providing services and the extent to which they improve outcomes for children in contact with social care services. We exclude services whose primary concern is with education, income support, housing, youth justice or health. We include services concerned with the well-being of children and families whether these are provided by the statutory, for profit or voluntary sectors. Most of the programme focused on services that have historically been provided by social services departments but there are also studies of services provided by the health service and by voluntary visitors.

The book itself is one of a number of research overviews known as 'messages from research'. Previous books have been written for practitioners and middle managers in social services. We believe the unusual topic of this overview makes it relevant to a wider audience. For example, as part of the consultation process we asked families for their opinions on what professionals should tell users about a service. They wanted to be told what a service offers and what its duties are; why staff think the service would help users; how long it has been running; what other parents got out of it and whether other parents would recommend it. It is hard to see that anyone involved at any level in social services should not be interested in such questions or, therefore, in what research has to say about them.

The two academic authors have had the support of an Advisory and Implementation Group made up of practitioners, managers, policy makers and researchers. The central aim of the book is to make messages from an important programme of studies more easily accessible to a wide audience and particularly to commissioners and managers in social care services for children. Before discussing these messages we need to say something about:

- the context within which the programme was commissioned
- the studies included in the programme
- the way they set out about their task
- the audiences for whom this book is intended.

The policy context

In 2003 the Government published the green paper *Every Child Matters* (HM Treasury 2003). The changes it proposed were radical. At its heart was a vision that was at once positive and inclusive. All children should be enabled to develop to their full potential. They should be healthy and safe. They should have fun. They should achieve. They should have economic well-being and they should make a positive contribution to society.

In reviewing current provision against these ideals the Government concentrated not so much on children's and young people's achievements or goals as on the challenges many of them face. It identified a variety of problems. Too many children and teenagers were truanting or in trouble with the law; too many were obese, bullied, pregnant, abused, homeless or witnesses to domestic violence; too many were abusing drugs, behaving in an anti-social way, failing to achieve at school or, if older, were unemployed and not receiving training or education. A plethora of agencies and initiatives had been attempting to tackle these problems. However, their efforts were not well co-ordinated and accountability was not clear. Children and families were still falling through the net. The help they received was often too little and too late.

The reforms encapsulated in *Every Child Matters* are intended to reduce these problems through a programme of early intervention and improved integration of front-line services, processes and strategies. The first steps have already been taken at the central and local government levels. There is now a Minister for Children with responsibility for a variety of functions previously held in different central government departments. In some local authorities, directors of children's services have already been appointed who have wide ranging responsibilities including Sure Start as well as services that have been provided through social services and education departments. There is a Children's Commissioner. The suggested children's trusts are intended to achieve further integration, bringing together local authority and health services for children and in some cases youth offending teams.

The aim is that there should be further integration at the level of practice. There are already pilot children's centres in which a number of previously disparate services operate from under one roof. There will be multi-disciplinary teams bringing together the skills of different professions. Schools will open for extended hours, offering their pupils a wide range of support after school is finished. Different agencies will be expected to use a common framework for assessment, develop protocols for exchanging information, and thus through the use of information technology eliminate the need for families to tell the same story to numerous different professionals.

These practice reforms will be accompanied by attention to the needs of the workforce. Proper workforce planning will help ensure that gaps will be filled and appropriate training is provided. Some common training will be available for all. So it is hoped, for example, that the provision of better training in issues relating to child abuse will reduce both the risks to children and the number of unnecessary referrals. In such ways, it is hoped, agencies will be less prone to 'pass the buck', better able to identify families in early need of help, more willing to offer help themselves, and better able to pass good information to each other when this is needed.

The research initiative began five years before the publication of *Every Child Matters*. Nevertheless the themes of the book resonate with the central concerns of *Every Child Matters* and findings have much to offer in the new context. Despite the changes, the essential functions or responsibilities that have fallen to local authorities remain. They do, however, have to be tackled in a new way. In all authorities, directors of children's services will be faced with the challenge of distributing their resources over a wide range of activities to move closer to the new policy requirements.

In meeting these requirements directors of children's services have to consider issues that were at the very heart of this initiative:

- how resources are distributed at the moment
- why they are distributed in this way
- what evidence there is of the effectiveness of the different services
- how to interpret this evidence
- what changes they are therefore in a position to make.

The new emphasis on early intervention poses these questions in a particularly acute way. How much of their resources should directors of children's services put into services delivered at an early point in a child's life that may prevent later difficulties? And how much do they have to reserve for those children who are already in very serious difficulties and for whom they have a particularly poignant responsibility?

Resource issues: an example

The green paper *Every Child Matters* estimated the annual cost of the 'Care System' at £2.2 billion. By contrast it estimates the cost of Connexions, the youth service, behaviour and education support teams, learning mentors and the children's fund at around £1 billion. Why is this distribution as it is? Could it be changed? Should it be changed?

The research findings can cast light on some of the likely effects and potential limitations of the programme of early intervention and service integration that is now proposed. Used thoughtfully, these findings can contribute to the debate about how best to use resources to support children. The findings from this initiative also allow us to make suggestions as to what kind of research – on both costs and effectiveness – should be carried out in future and what methods it can use.

Before discussing the research findings we need to give brief details of the studies themselves, look at some of the key concepts used in the research, at the methods it used, and at the implications of all this for the way the research is understood.

The studies

All but one of the studies formed part of the original Department of Health initiative. This asked researchers to design studies that either described the use of resources or alternatively compared the costs and effectiveness of services for similar or overlapping populations. The researchers were expected to build on previous knowledge but also to add this new perspective. Thus in contrast to previous initiatives all studies were expected to include an economic component. In this way it was hoped that alliances would be formed between social researchers and economists and that recommendations would no longer be presented without any consideration of their cost.

The resulting research proposals were peer reviewed for their technical merit and their policy relevance. A commissioning group at the Department of Health made the final choice, seeking to produce a balanced group of studies that would cover a wide field.

The economic component

Previous studies of children's social care services hardly ever included an economic component and were rarely concerned with effects. Their explanations and recommendations have thus excluded an economic perspective. By contrast all 14 studies in this programme include an economic component and many also focus on effects. The recommendations in *Every Child Matters*, particularly those concerned with the need for more 'early' intervention, imply a shift of resources. They also imply that in some sense this will be 'more effective'. The programme is therefore particularly relevant to this new vision of social care.

The Home-Start study was not funded by Central Government but commissioned by the Joseph Rowntree Foundation. It formed part of an initiative concerned with the costs and outcomes of preventive services, so the results would be highly relevant to this initiative. The commissioning process was analogous to that used by the Department of Health. The principal researcher joined with other researchers in a programme of seminars on the common challenges all faced.

Overall the book covers 14 studies. Table 1.1 at the end of this chapter, gives brief details about each study's design and the measures used where they are relevant to our interpretation of the findings. We give the name we will use for the study in this overview and each study has a number that is used when we want to refer briefly to one or more studies that cover a particular topic. A numbered list is also given in Appendix B showing the full project title.

Table 1.1 shows just how widely the studies range across service settings and across groups of children and young people. In this respect the review contrasts with earlier ones, for example on adoption, in which a single issue has been tackled in several studies. An advantage of this breadth is that the initiative can cast light on the use of resources in a wide variety of different contexts. This diversity also means that findings should be compared and contrasted carefully as no two studies cover exactly the same area. To overcome this, we have selected findings that will cast light on overarching themes and those that will be of interest to commissioners and managers in the new mix of children's social care services.

This strategy means that we have not reported all the detailed findings from any given study. We recommend that readers with an interest in a particular topic view the researchers' own summaries at www.everychildmatters.gov.uk. Contact information for the lead researcher is also on this web page. Each individual study also carefully embeds its findings in previous research findings. We have reported rather little of this contextual information. In order to keep the book to a reasonable

Overarching themes

- To what extent can these studies help commissioners and providers understand the implications of their decision?
- What do the various services and supports cost?
- How do children and young people use services and supports, and at what cost?
- Do these services improve outcomes for children and young people, and are they effective?
- Can preventative services avert the problems on which social services traditionally spend a high proportion of their resources?
- Which early intervention services are good investments?
- Are there better ways of spending money on later interventions?
- How can the challenges of collaboration be met?

length we have made considerable use of material in earlier 'messages from research' overviews to help interpret some of the current studies' findings within a much longer stream of research.

We make one further comment. Issues of diversity are high on the agenda for children's social care services yet we say little about them. Many of the studies have addressed the young people's different experiences through interviews. Nevertheless the quantitative analysis has been limited to assessing impacts on broad groupings of people. This is because statistical analysis requires large numbers. Researchers recognise that there is a vast range of peoples, cultures, religions and histories covered under, for example, the label 'Chinese', but in most studies there will only be one or two 'Chinese' people.[1] To allow statistical analysis, most studies group them together with other Black and Ethnic Minority people.

For similar reasons all disabled children have commonly been put in one group. This makes little allowance for the potentially very different experiences of those with, for example, profound intellectual impairment or mild learning difficulties. The researchers recognise these are crude groupings. The general assumption is that these heterogeneous groups may share common experiences, for example

---

1   In theory very large studies could overcome this problem. In practice, however, the numbers would have to be very large indeed and would probably be bought at a price in terms of either the depth or the range of information collected. The secondary analysis of the Children in Need survey is one of the few studies to explore service use and costs by disaggregated groups of ethnic groupings or different disabilities (Department for Education and Skills 2001).

racism or the limitations imposed by society's reactions to disability. Here we only report instances where the larger studies showed service receipt or cost differences associated with ethnic grouping and disability. However, we urge readers to explore what the studies have to report from the young people themselves.

Key concepts

The research programme focused on children in difficulty. It tried to describe their needs, the outcomes they achieved, and the costs and effects of the services delivered to them. These concepts of 'difficulty', 'need', 'outcome', and 'effects' and 'cost' are slippery. Different people use them in different ways. Rather than suggest there is a correct way, it is easier to describe how we will use them in the book.

As we use them, the concepts relate to the 'reasonable state of health or development' that is invoked in by the Children Act 1989 in its definition of a 'child in need'. For the purposes of this Act a child in need is one who is either disabled or unlikely to reach or maintain this 'reasonable state' without the provision of services by the local authority. Put briefly:

- A *difficulty* is anything that either marks the absence of this 'reasonable state' (such as poor health) or makes it hard to achieve (for example, poor housing).[2]

- A *need* is a difficulty that is assessed as requiring a particular service or intervention if this reasonable state is to be reached or maintained (so an inability to read may be assessed as requiring special tuition if a child is to develop to their full capacity).

- *Outcomes* concern the degree to which the needs are met (that is whether a reasonable state has been reached or maintained). We often use the term *well-being* as an overarching term for the many domains over which outcomes have been assessed in any study. In general the outcomes discussed in the research are related to but more specific than the five broad outcomes identified in *Every Child Matters*.

- An *effect* is an outcome that is produced by a service. It is judged comparatively. So an effective service is one that is more effective than another or than no service at all.

- *Cost*, as used in this book, refers to the financial costs associated with providing services.

---

2   In this sense 'a difficulty' is not precisely the same as a 'risk factor'. The latter essentially marks out a group that is likely to have poor outcomes. A risk factor may or may not be a difficulty as we define it although obviously the two are often the same.

As we use the words, the key difference between effects and outcomes lies in whether or not we are talking about cause and effect. Outcomes may be associated with interventions but are not necessarily caused by them. If we talk about the effects of an intervention we are implying a causal relationship.[3]

The emphasis on these key concepts marks this initiative out from earlier ones. As we will see in later chapters, the focus of much previous research in children's social care services has been the assessment and description of children's *difficulties* and *needs*. Some of these earlier studies have also looked at *outcomes* either in relation to the children's needs being met, or the extent to which children have attained one or more of the 'global' outcomes recommended by current policy or encapsulated in performance indicators.

What makes this initiative different is that it encouraged researchers to look at *effectiveness* and to look at *costs*. In a few studies, researchers were able to bring these concepts together and measure cost-effectiveness, or measure the associations between costs and outcomes. Measuring these components is technically difficult. In Chapter 2 we give more detail on how researchers in this initiative have overcome these challenges.

The questions addressed

The studies we discuss fall into three broad groups. Some are essentially 'analytic descriptive'. They describe, for example, the costs of different services, the length of time episodes of service last or the views of children. A second group of studies compares different kinds of services or a particular service against 'service as usual', for example, special as against routine home visiting. The general aim of these studies is to see if one kind of service is cheaper or more effective than another serving a similar clientele. A third group of studies is concerned with comparing different services or units of the same general type, for example, children's homes. The aim here is to identify aspects of the service that make for a more effective service – perhaps a high staff ratio – after allowing for differences in the kinds of children served.

Each of these different kinds of study makes a distinctive contribution. The descriptive analytic studies follow a long tradition of research in children social care services. In this initiative they have an added value as all have a costs component. Some develop unit costs for different services, perhaps the cost per day for

---

3   Effects, like outcomes, apply to both individuals and broader groups. So it is possible to take repeated measures of, say, the educational performance of children in secondary schools without implying what produced any changes. Equally it is possible to speak about the impact of, say, changes in the law on sentencing policy. In the case of this book, however, the analysis of effects almost invariably applies to individuals.

EBD schools,[4] or for different social work teams, or for assessments. Other studies calculate the support costs per child: how much is spent on this child or this group of children. Many go on to explore why the costs of supporting children vary: is this variation related to their characteristics or difficulties? Or does it have more to do with the service responses?

The second group of studies involves comparing two (at least) ways of doing something and asking whether one achieves better outcomes for children and young people than another. For example the Adolescent Prevention and Home-Start studies compare the costs and outcomes for users of two different services that serve a similar population. By looking at young people just before they use the service and then assessing them again after a certain period of time, these studies seek to identify the impact of the service. The aim is to see whether one service can generate better outcomes for children and if so whether this is at the same, less or greater cost.

The third group of studies makes comparisons *within* a service category. That is, they look at a particular service – say adoption or family support services – across several providers and use statistical techniques to explore whether particular processes or characteristics of the service have an impact on outcomes or on costs. This kind of study is of value to those who have to decide how to run particular services. For example, it may be useful to know that late adoptions are less successful than ones made earlier or that children's homes with high staff ratios do not seem more successful than ones with lower ratios.

Irrespective of the kind of study involved the same questions tend to recur.

1. What is money being spent on?

   This type of question recurs in all the broad types of study outlined above.

2. What makes a service more effective?

   This type of question is clearly of central concern to the comparative studies. Implicitly, however, it is of interest in the analytic studies as well. As an example, these studies typically contain information on children's views. It is hard to see how decisions on whether a service 'works' can be taken without taking these views into account.

3. How far is one service more cost-effective than another?

   Essentially this involves bringing answers to the previous two questions together. Again this issue is of more obvious concern to the comparative studies. Equally, however, a balanced judgement to prefer one service

---

4   EBD schools are special schools for pupils with emotional or behavioural difficulties (EBD). The term behavioural, emotional and social difficulties (BESD) has recently been adopted.

rather than another has to take account of the kind of information generated by the descriptive analytic studies. Basic descriptive information on how money is spent, what children and their parent(s) think of services, and what happens to those who receive it provides an essential context for judging a service.

These questions are sensible but unfortunately not easy to answer. The reasons for the difficulty are partly technical. It is, for example, hard to show that a service has an effect or that, if it does, this effect could be easily reproduced elsewhere. In Chapter 2 we discuss some of the approaches researchers have used to tackle these technical problems. In part, however, the difficulties have to do with issues of ethics and judgement. In order to judge effects we have to decide on what is to count as an outcome: a change in a child's behaviour, maybe? Or perhaps helping parents over a difficult patch? We may have to decide what weight to give to one outcome as against another. We also have to take into account the degree of uncertainty that inevitably belongs to even the most clear-cut results.

In the end, and despite the uncertainties, judgements have to be made on how best to support children and families. These judgements have to take account of professional opinion, user views and local and national policy – a broad sweep of considerations, requirements and aspirations that is in turn informed by a myriad of political, practical and professional concerns. They also have to take account of research. This book acknowledges the uncertainties but its central task is to point to the ways the research can be used.

Who should read this book?

We hope that a wide variety of groups will find this book of interest. In writing it, however, we have had in mind four main groups:

- those who commission services and who need to know about the context within which these services are provided, how they operate and are perceived, and the comparative costs and effects of different kinds of service
- those who provide services who also need feedback on the operation of their services and are likely to be particularly concerned with the characteristics of services likely to produce the best result given their budget
- practitioners who need information of the above kinds to inform the decisions they take and provide 'ammunition' in the arguments they make
- researchers and students who need a quick overview of the research as a preliminary to more detailed study.

These groups are likely to read the book with rather different eyes. For this reason we have placed material that will be of interest to only some readers in footnotes where others can safely ignore them. That said, we hope that all the groups read the book with an eye that is at once realistic and positive. In this way they can acknowledge the uncertainties but move beyond them to use the research to inform their decisions.

One final point should be made in this section. This overview is based on a rich and successful set of studies. It is also highly selective. It is not possible to include all the points that apply to the particular services studied in the research. For many purposes there is no substitute for reading the studies themselves.

Conclusion

This book faces the challenge of showing how the answers to questions studied in an earlier era can be relevant to a new one. We have argued that this is possible. The questions addressed in this research are central to the new vision of children's social care services. This book should allow those shaping services for children to see how their resources have been deployed. This in turn should allow them to consider how these resources might be redeployed in the future. In this second phase of their deliberations it would help if they knew why the resources had been used as they were, how realistic it was to think that collaboration and early intervention will save money, how much different services cost and how effective they were. These are the issues with which this book is concerned.

Overall, therefore, our aim is to outline a body of research that is accessible and that will assist those leading, planning, commissioning and delivering social care and other multi-agency services for children and their families. In the current context of children's services, this book should help partner agencies to discuss how their resources could be used to best effect in achieving the *Change for Children* (DfES 2004) agenda locally and in a way that seeks to maximise the improvements in outcomes for children and their families.

Readers can find the full text of this book, along with related material including the executive summary, stakeholder reports, researcher summaries and leaflets at www.everychildmatters.gov.uk/socialcare.

Summary

The programme of research on the *Costs and Effectiveness of Services for Children in Need*, supported by the Department of Health and the Department for Education and Skills, focuses on the way child social care services are delivered, the costs of providing those services and the extent to which they improve outcomes for children. The 14 studies cover a diverse range of topics from supporting families with young children in their own homes to looking at staff motivations and skills in services for children looked after by local authorities. The chapter explains the key concepts of *difficulty*, *need*, *outcomes*, *effects* and *costs* and highlights some of the research designs employed. In general the outcomes discussed in the research concern the degree to which the needs are met. They are related to but more specific than the five broad outcomes identified in *Every Child Matters*. Each study is briefly described in Table 1.1. This introduction to the overview also outlines the policy background for child social care services today allowing us to select findings from these studies that will cast light on overarching themes relevant to commissioners and providers as they implement the *Change for Children* agenda.

Table 1.1 The *Costs and Effectiveness* studies: design and techniques for assessment and analysis

No.	Short title	Authors	Overall design	Assessing costs	Assessing needs and outcomes	Analysis of costs, needs and outcome
1	Health Visiting study	J. Barlow S. Stewart-Brown H. Davis E. Mackintosh S. Kirkpatrick P. Jarrett C. Mockford	Compares a new Intensive Health Visiting service with routine practice for 120 vulnerable mothers-to-be using a randomised controlled trial design. One-year follow-up from entry to the service.	Support package costs estimated from interview data on public sector[1] service use. 'Willingness to pay' survey of primary school parents.	Standardised quantitative measures of parent/child well-being. Semi-structured interviews with health visitors and mothers.	CEA[2] including incremental cost-effective ratios (ICER)[3] and cost-effectiveness acceptability curves. CBA[4] using willingness to pay approach.
2	Costs of Children in Need study	A. Bebbington J. Beecham	Secondary analysis of the national one week SSD survey of *Children in Need (CIN) 2001*.	CIN survey data cleaned: SSD support costs per week for 177,570 (83%) of those receiving services in the survey week.	Data available from the CIN survey on children's characteristics and membership of one of nine 'need groups'.	Statistical estimation of the links[5] between SSD costs, children's characteristics and needs, and LA characteristics.
3	Troubled Adolescents study	D. Berridge J. Beecham I. Brodie T. Cole H. Daniels M. Knapp V. MacNeill	Develops methods to combine education and social care perspectives. Exploratory analysis compares 257 adolescents living in EBD schools, children's homes, and foster care linked to four LAs.	Develops methodology for estimating comprehensive and comparable unit costs for children's homes and EBD schools.	Qualitative and quantitative data on the three types of services[6] and children's needs. Case studies of six young people.	Characteristics, needs, and costs are each described and compared across the service types.

Continued on next page

Table 1.1 cont.

No.	Short title	Authors	Overall design	Assessing costs	Assessing needs and outcomes	Analysis of costs, needs and outcome
4	Adolescent Prevention study	N. Biehal S. Byford H. Weatherly	Compares Specialist Adolescent Support Teams and mainstream social work in eight LAs for 195 young people at risk of admission to care. Six-month follow-up from entry to the service.	Support package costs estimated from interview data on public sector service use.	Standardised and new quantitative measures of child and family well-being. 50 in-depth children's interviews.	CEA including ICER. Statistical estimation of the links between costs and children's characteristics, needs, and outcomes.
5	Therapeutic Family Support (TFS) study	J. Carpenter J. Tidmarsh J. Slade J. Schneider P. Coolen-Schrijner D. Woof	Explores variation in the costs and outcomes of 21 TFS services for 61 young families. Six-month follow-up from entry to the service.	Estimation of unit costs *within* FSS. Support package costs estimated from interview data on public sector service use.	Standardised quantitative measures of child and family well-being.	Statistical estimation of the links between costs and children's characteristics, needs, and outcomes, and service characteristics.
6	Assessment Framework study	H. Cleaver S. Walker P. Meadows	Explores the impact of the implementation of the Assessment Framework and records in 24 SSDs.	Estimates the unit cost of a core assessment including consultation with and attendance by non-SSD professionals.	Structured interviews with managers, practitioners and families. Audit of 2248 referrals.	No statistical analysis. Core assessment costs set in the context of audit and LA practices.
7	Care Leavers study	J. Dixon J. Wade S. Byford H. Weatherly J. Lee	Explores arrangements, outcomes and costs for 106 young people supported by seven Leaving Care Teams. 10–18 month follow-up from entry to service.	Support package costs estimated from interview data on public and independent sector service use.	Standardised quantitative measures of child well-being. Semi-structured interviews with managers, workers and young people.	Statistical estimation of the links between costs and children's characteristics, needs, and outcomes, and service characteristics.

8	Children's Homes study	L. Hicks I. Gibbs S. Byford H. Weatherly	Describes the practice of 45 children's homes' managers, and assesses its impact on the 301 staff, the care environments, and 175 current residents who were re-interviewed one year later.	Using data from finance depts, a unit cost (per resident week) is estimated for each home; one for the home itself and one that includes costs for 'off site' services used residents.	Quantitative postal questionnaires to staff, social workers and residents. Visits to all homes and staff group discussions in ten homes. Qualitative telephone interviews with managers.	Statistical estimation of the links between unit costs per week, residents' needs and outcomes, leadership, strategies, and sector.
9	Child Protection study	I. Katz S. Bhabra J. Corlyon P. Moran D. Ghate V. La Placa J. Beecham	Explores the way social services and child and adolescent mental health services (CAMHS) link at organisational (five LAs), service, and child-levels (3 LAs and 234 children).	Use a range of sources to identify CAMHS expenditure in the five LAs. Estimates unit costs for child protection conferences and reviews.	Quantitative data from case files and a standardised measure of mental health. Semi-structured interviews with senior managers, 19 parents and 15 young people.	No statistical analysis with cost data. Reviews the economic evidence on the interface between CAMHS and the child protection system.
10	Foster Carer study	D. Kirton J. Beecham K. Ogilvie	Explores the links between foster care expenditure and performance in 149 LAs, and key actors attitudes to and satisfaction with the different levels and systems of payments.	Local authority data on actual and proportionate expenditure and the foster care unit cost are taken from the Key Statistics Returns.	Qualitative data from focus groups in 16 LAs and five IFAs. Quantitative data from a survey of 1181 foster carers working in these agencies, and the agencies themselves.	Statistical estimation of the links between foster care expenditure and performance indicators in 149 LAs.

Continued on next page

Table 1.1 cont.

No.	Short title	Authors	Overall design	Assessing costs	Assessing needs and outcomes	Analysis of costs, needs and outcome
11	Home-Start study	C. McAuley M. Knapp J. Beecham N. McCurry M. Sleed	Comparative study of the costs and effects of Home-Start and routinely provided services. 162 young families with a 12-month follow-up from entry to service.	Support package costs estimated from interview data on public sector service use.	At outset and follow-up: standardised quantitative measures of child and family well-being; semi-structured interviews with all mothers.	Comparison of average costs and outcomes.[7] Statistical estimation of the links between costs, characteristics, needs, and outcomes.
12	Sexual Abuse study	P. McCrone T. Weeramanthri M. Knapp A. Rushton J. Trowell G. Miles I. Kolvin	Compares the costs and effectiveness of group and individual therapy for young girls who have been sexually abused.	Focuses on the costs of therapy including associated activities such as the introductory meeting, assessment, carer support and therapist supervision.	Standardised quantitative measures of child and family well-being. (The outcomes study was completed before the cost-effectiveness study was funded.)	Comparison of average costs and outcomes.
13	Adoption study	J. Selwyn W. Sturgess D. Quinton C. Baxter	Examines the costs and outcomes over time for 130 children who were approved for adoption in one LA between 1991–6.	Unit costs estimated for placing child for adoption, and maintaining the placement pre- and post adoption. Some family costs identified. Costs of delay and care careers calculated.	Standardised quantitative measures of child and family well-being completed during 2002. Case files reviewed. Interviews with 87 adoptive or foster carers.	The costs for the adoption processes are set in the context of LA practices. Down-stream placement costs estimated for those with unstable care careers.

| 14 | Care Careers study | H. Ward
L. Holmes
J. Soper
R. Olsen | Explores social care support for purposive sample of looked after children in six LAs. Designs an EXCEL programme to calculate SSD 'per child' costs over time. | Estimates unit costs for eight social work processes.

SSD costs for a 20-month period are estimated for 478 young people. | Data from management information systems and case files on the children's characteristic and needs.

Qualitative interviews with 47 children and young people. | Compares the costs for children grouped by broad dimensions of need. Explores associations between needs, costs and experiences. |

Notes

1 Public sector perspective includes all services likely to be funded from public expenditure sources: social care services, health services, education, youth justice, as well as services provided through voluntary or private sector organisations. Includes housing, employment-related services and social security where relevant for the study population.

2 CEA – cost effectiveness analysis.

3 The additional cost of an outcome.

4 CBA – cost-benefit analysis.

5 Often called a cost function analysis. This form of analysis also has the potential to explore cost-effectiveness through multiple outcomes.

6 Almost all the studies described the services under study. Here, the focus was on comparing the organisation and care environment of EBD schools and children's homes; two services with very different aims.

7 The cost and outcome findings from studies 11 and 12 could be plotted the in 'cost-effectiveness quadrants' in a way that meant further analysis to show cost-effectiveness was unnecessary.

Chapter 2

How the Studies Were Done

Introduction

This chapter is about method: in other words about how the studies were done. In pointing this out we may already have lost many of our readers. For those who lack the time to read this chapter we have tried to ensure that the remaining ones make sense on their own. We hope, however, that most will read on. We argued in Chapter 1 that actions based on research have to take account both of the certainty of the conclusions and of more general considerations. In this way research is not an alternative to public debate but can inform it. This, however, can only happen if a wide range of people understands the nature of the evidence research supplies.

In discussing the methods and hence the nature of the evidence we have concentrated on three key tasks:

- assessing costs
- assessing effects
- bringing together costs and effects.

Assessing costs

Assessing costs was a central part of the initiative. Costs are difficult to estimate and to date have rarely been featured in children's social care research. One challenge in taking an economic perspective is that words in everyday use – cost, price, etc. – have specific technical meanings. In this overview *costs* mean financial costs: items that can be valued using money. That is not to say we are ignoring the personal costs of a distressing situation, just that these are included in the difficulty and need domains identified in Chapter 1.

Many of these studies use two broad types of costs: first, the unit costs of services and second, but building on the first, the costs of supporting a child – their care package costs.

Unit costs 'summarise' the amount of resources (staff, buildings and equipment, for example) absorbed to produce a unit of output for that service. These 'output units' often make use of time periods of service: a day in a placement, an hour of social work, a session in a day nursery, etc. One example of how a unit cost might be estimated is the Performance Assessment Framework (PAF) indicator on unit costs for residential care. Here, the total amount spent per year on residential care is divided by the total number of places in the homes and the number of weeks in the year. This is a 'top-down' calculation that gives the average cost per resident day for that local authority.

Most of the studies in this initiative have taken a much more detailed approach to estimating unit costs and looked at specific facilities. For example, they describe a particular children's home and add up all the amounts spent on staff, heating, food, and so on, going into it. Then this total is divided by the number of places in the home and the number of weeks it is open. This 'bottom-up' approach usually gives a more accurate cost for any particular service. It can, for example, show that different children's homes – or other services studied – have different costs. Not all services within the same category have the same unit cost, even if they are based in the same local authority (see Chapter 4). From a cost perspective, one of the most important parts of the research reports lies in their description of how costs were estimated. This allows others to repeat the methodology, perhaps for different years or for different geographical areas.

The PAF unit costs and those estimated in these studies may be different, perhaps because of the level of detail used, or because slightly different components are included. Generally in these studies, unit cost estimates include on-site recurrent expenditure (staff salaries, office expenditure, food and the like), direct management costs, and the cost implications of any buildings, equipment or other capital.[1] This is closer to the total recovery cost model often used by non-public sector organisations when 'pricing' their services for contracts. PAF unit costs are more likely to use only recurrent expenditure for any given year, and when looking at the costs of particular services, local authorities' unit costs might only include the direct 'on-site' recurrent expenditure.

Another reason why unit costs may differ concerns the issue of 'costs to whom'. In estimating unit costs, PAF indicators and some studies in this initiative only look at costs to social services. As more jointly funded services come on stream, a wider view will be needed. For example, some of the Home-Start services were part-funded by social services departments and part-funded by the local NHS Trust. So if only social services' funding is counted then costs of the Home-Start service

---

1   This unit cost then reflects the costs of increasing the capacity of the system by one place, rather than squeezing another child into the existing capacity. The unit cost reflects the need to build new buildings or increase management capacity as more children use the service (see Beecham 2000). In all these studies, unit cost estimation was guided by this approach.

would be underestimated, perhaps by as much as a half. Thus, a *public sector* perspective is common in this research.

Costs for when? This is another overarching question. Again it is complex. Accountants commonly use costs per annum. For most of the research in this initiative the unit costs reflect the 'units of service' that a young person will use (per hour, per day, etc.) However there is another time dimension to consider. For example, the Troubled Adolescent study compared the unit costs of a week in EBD schools and children's homes. The former seemed a cheaper option. But by taking a longer-term view a different picture emerged. Young people were likely to attend EBD schools for a number of years but residence in children's homes typically lasted only a few weeks or months. Either placement might be appropriate for a given child, but knowledge about the potential longer-term costs and impacts should also influence decisions about how money is spent today.

Questions to ask about costs

Assessing costs for individual services can be complex and time-consuming but are far more informative than broad average data. Many of the studies have made a major contribution to developing methodologies and estimates of the costs of social care services. Questions to ask about cost estimates include:

- Costs for what? What items have been included?

- Costs to whom? The costs to which agencies have been included?

- Costs for when? Over what time period does this cost span?

This leads us quite naturally to the second way costs are presented in these studies; the notion of a cost per child. Each child will use not just one service but several concurrently. A young person in residential care may also see their social worker and see a GP for health checks. Many children in these studies used education services, whether mainstream school or more specialist provision. Many also needed support from mental health services. To add to the complexity, each child will use different amounts of each service (including not using it) depending on their needs. By multiplying the amount of each service used by its unit cost and then adding these together, the cost per child – or more accurately the cost of each child's care package – can be calculated. Again, measurement can be limited to just social services – as with the Children in Need surveys. A wider perspective would include education, health, housing, youth justice, etc. It could also include services provided by for-profit or non-profit organisations which can be funded by parents or carers, or by public sector organisations.

The studies recorded care package components over different periods. The Cost of Children in Need study, for example, uses a one-week survey of all children receiving social services support. The Care Careers study used the longest follow-up period at 20 months. Generally, the longer the period over which service use is recorded, the greater the support costs for that young person.

In economic evaluation the ideal is to consider the relevant costs to all parts of society, regardless of who bears them. The service use and costs data should cover the same period for which outcomes are measured. In reality the perspective taken in any study is dependent on the research questions asked, on the service context and on the research resources available.

Assessing outcomes and effects

The great majority of United Kingdom research on social care services for children, and indeed research from many other countries, has not been designed either to cost services or assess effects. This generalisation is certainly true of the research included in earlier 'messages from research' overviews that have commonly used interviews with families and descriptions of children's difficulties, views and careers as foundations for their important messages. For example, the studies have consistently pointed to the poor educational performance of looked after children. Some older children who have left the care system also lamented the lack of attention to their education. So it was natural to recommend that greater attention should be paid to the education of looked after children and that care services should collaborate with education departments. As later educational attainment depends heavily on successful first steps, it is easy to argue that such collaboration should begin early. These notions are now firmly entrenched in policy on children's services.

Studies of the kind described above are relevant to the way resources are used. In many cases they are essential preliminaries to more evaluative research. The recommendation that children who are looked after should receive special attention at school is certainly reasonable in the light of the research. Despite this apparent rationality the first attempts to improve education may prove costly, distort priorities and result in no improvement at all.[2] A full evaluation would require attention to both costs and effects.

---

2   This could be for a number of reasons: those entering the care system may be so far behind with their education that only a massive intervention will enable them to catch up; the techniques used to implement these interventions may be ineffective; the children may prove less keen on their education than had been hoped.

In practice the evaluation of the costs and effects of services is not a neat and tidy business. It is technically difficult, involves ethical and political decisions, and rarely provides clear-cut conclusions. Instead researchers evaluating a service unsteadily feel their way towards answers to a number of key questions.

- What are the key characteristics of the actual and potential recipients?
- What is the content of and context for the service?
- What are the costs of the service?
- What kinds (domains) of outcomes should be measured?
- What are the associations between elements of the service, the costs and the outcomes?

Answers to the first four questions require the kind of 'descriptive analytic' approach that has been traditional in this area. As will be seen, much of the research in this programme is essentially – and rightly – descriptive. It is, however, the attempt to assess and relate costs and effects, and to relate costs to needs and outcomes, which marks out this initiative as distinctive. In this respect the 'answers' it provides are subject to various sources of uncertainty and they do not have the benefit of a body of previous work in which to set the findings.

As discussed in Chapter 1 the first source of uncertainty is that all the questions themselves are framed in the light of values and judgements about which there may be dispute. For public sector services, what counts as a need is determined partly by moral or political views about what entitles a person to support. It also reflects ideas about what will help meet that need, the broad level of expenditure, the nature of the outcomes to be achieved, and the likelihood that a given service will result in these outcomes. Similarly the definition of 'key elements' in a service (for example, within residential care) depends on ideas about which elements contribute either to cost or to the outcomes it is intended to achieve.

Judgements and values are particularly closely involved in creating measures of outcome. The values implied by these outcome measures are typically those held by practitioners or researchers. Recipients may hold other values. For example, some parents may welcome an admission to the care system, whereas practitioners may seek to prevent it. Services that are highly responsive to their users are also likely to pursue a wide variety of different aims. This creates problems for researchers, who are unlikely to be able to measure all the desired outcomes.[3] As will be seen in this

---

3   A service for families in difficulty might tackle problems of debt, housing, depression, domestic violence, drug addiction, difficult teenagers, endlessly crying babies and much else besides. A relatively small number of people might be helped in relation to each of these problems. As a result it may be difficult to show that this service was more effective than another in tackling any of these problems.

overview it is not uncommon to find services that are popular with their users but that cannot be shown to have other obvious effects. The technical difficulties of measuring an outcome precisely, and the breadth of the domains on which a service may have an impact, substantially increase the problem of identifying effects.

A second source of uncertainty lies in the nature of the techniques used to assess effectiveness. To say that a service is effective in an absolute sense is, in most cases, to say that it brings about an outcome that would not have occurred had the service not been provided. In practice similar individuals often receive different services, while some who receive a service are similar to others who get no service at all.

Researchers can seek to exploit this 'natural variation' in order to see whether some services are more effective than others. The challenge is that in practice there tends to be differences as well as similarities between those getting one service and those getting another and that these differences may explain part or all of the differences in outcome between these services.[4]

Some considerations in research design

Studies that compare the effects of services are difficult. How can researchers know that apparently effective services are not simply dealing with less difficult problems? How can they be sure that apparently good effects are likely to be repeated elsewhere?

In dealing with these difficulties researchers typically rely on:

- *description*: the careful description of sampling, samples and services

- *design*: designs that use matching or statistical techniques to 'control for intake' or that randomly allocate recipients between different options

- *statistical significance*: the likelihood that differences would occur by chance

- *explicitness* about the assumptions behind measures of outcome, about the measures themselves and about the size of differences.

These precautions undoubtedly reduce the problem but do not do away with the need for judgement in assessing results.

---

4   The comparisons are made in terms of factors that increase or lower the probability of certain outcomes. Even if all the relevant factors were known the outcomes would still not be fully predictable. Subsequent events that could not be predicted or 'chaotic' features of the processes involved could still tip the balance between good and bad outcomes. The assumption is that these processes would be equally prevalent on both sides of a comparison. The problem arises when not all the relevant factors are known and one of the 'unknowns' is more prevalent in one of the comparison groups than another. In the example given here, difficulties that occur randomly in a population are likely to attract social work visits that are therefore in themselves a marker of problems.

Most of the research reviewed in this book has used statistical methods to overcome this problem. In essence this involves predicting how well a set of individuals are likely to do given their initial characteristics. It is then possible to see if those who get a particular service do better or worse than would be predicted. This approach has the problem that the researchers may not have taken account of all the relevant characteristics of those receiving the intervention. To give a simple example, social workers are more likely to pay frequent visits to families about whom they are worried. A probable consequence is that frequent visits are associated with worse outcomes, and this result may remain even when other family characteristics are taken into account. It would be very wrong to conclude that frequent visits 'cause' bad outcomes, or that they are less effective than no visits at all.

Faced with these difficulties two of the sets of researchers in this initiative set up 'randomised controlled trials'. Essentially this involves taking control of the intake to two or more contrasting services and allocating users to each service as it were 'through the toss of a coin'. This approach has the major advantage of enabling an estimate to be made of the likelihood that two services differ in their ability to produce a given change. It also has limitations. It can present practical and ethical difficulties. It does not, in itself, identify which of the complex ingredients in a service contribute to any success or which aspects of the context are essential. For these reasons it is difficult to be certain about what would happen if the context, staff, service or recipients were very slightly different or an experimental intervention were implemented more widely in ordinary contexts.

A third source of uncertainty has to do with probability. Here there are two different ways in which research results may mislead. First, results may suggest that there is an effect when in fact one intervention has merely, as it were, 'had a good day'; if a larger sample were to be collected the apparent difference would disappear.[5] Second, researchers generally only report results when they would have appeared by chance less than 1 in 20 times (in the jargon they are statistically significant).[6] This self-imposed restraint increases the chance of an opposite error. Researchers may believe that a service is not effective when a larger sample would have shown that it was. Failure to provide evidence that a service is effective does not, of itself, show that the service is ineffective.

---

5   This is sometimes referred to as 'statistical power'. There are a number of websites that allow the required sample size to be calculated. See, for example, DSS Research 2005.

6   Even this wise precaution may fail to ensure against error. If investigating an unfamiliar area the researcher may need to investigate a large number of possible associations. The greater the number of tests carried out, the greater the chance that one or other of them will be significant. Allowances can be made for this possibility. Strictly speaking most of the findings in this kind of exploratory research have to be regarded as plausible hypotheses.

Researchers try to be explicit about the nature of these uncertainties, while also reducing them as far as possible. They also form judgements about the most likely explanation of their findings in the light of the accepted uncertainties. Ideally this interpretation of results is internally coherent, is in keeping with other research, and also fits with common sense, relevant theory and professional opinion. Even in these favourable circumstances the judgements remain uncertain. So researchers regard it as good practice to hedge their conclusions with caveats and alternative possibilities.

Unfortunately practitioners and managers cannot afford too much of this luxury of doubt. Leaving things as they are is in itself a form of action. Inevitably therefore practitioners have to act. In doing so they are wise if they form a view of the most likely consequence of their actions. In writing this book we have therefore tried both to highlight the pervasive uncertainty in the findings and also to point busy managers and practitioners towards what we see as the most likely interpretation.[7]

Bringing costs, outcomes and effects together

Many of the decisions taken by commissioners or managers will reflect considerations of cost as well as likely effects. Economics has a similar scope of interests. In evaluative research it offers a variety of ways of combining costs and outcome or effectiveness information to help inform decision-making (see Box 2.1). Each will provide different types of information. The complexity of children's services means that findings from all of these evaluation types can be useful in developing policy and provision.

Box 2.1 Types of economic evaluation

In all analyses, a comprehensive view of costs is advocated so that all relevant resources (costs) are measured, regardless of where they fall.

Cost cost-minimisation cost-offset analysis

Outcomes assumed to be similar between the groups but not measured.

---

7   In practice it is perfectly rational for managers and practitioners to choose to act as if a less likely interpretation was correct. This is because they have to consider not only the likelihood of a given result but also the costs and benefits of being right or wrong. It may be wise to guard against an unlikely outcome if its occurrence would be disastrous. After all it is not irrational for people to use insurance companies and not surprising that these companies make money.

Cost-effectiveness analysis

A single outcome measure is used. The ratio between costs and effectiveness (cost per unit of improvement) is often calculated.

Cost-utility analysis

Can be thought of as a special category of cost-effectiveness. Quality Adjusted Life Years (QALYs) or Disability Adjusted Life Years (DALYs) are common measure in health economics but CUA in social care is very limited. The Older People's Utility Scale (OPUS) is an example of a utility measure for older people, but there are none to date in child social care.

Cost-consequences analysis

Employs multiple outcomes. Results are not as clear-cut as when using the single outcomes analysis but may provide a closer reflection of the multiple aims of child social care services.

Cost-benefit analysis

Outcomes and costs are measured in the same metric. This would require, for example, valuing a change in behaviour in money. Willingness to pay methodologies are being developed.

Many researchers in this initiative estimate unit costs for services and use them to calculate the costs of care packages for children and young people in the study. This is the first stage of many economic evaluations. Where measures of costs and effects were brought together, cost-effectiveness analysis was the most common approach. Four studies met the requirements for a cost-effectiveness study in that they compared at least two service options or one option against 'service as usual'; the Health Visiting (1), Adolescent Prevention (4), Home-Start (11), and Sexual Abuse (12) studies. Each assessed costs and needs as the young people began to use the services being studied, and they assessed costs and outcomes (changes in needs) at a follow-up interview. The comparative element allowed the researchers to assess which was the more cost-effective option.

Two of these studies employed 'decision-rules' to assess whether one option was more cost-effective than another (studies 11 and 12). These decision rules are questions that link costs and effects: Does this service produce the same level of outcomes as the other service but at less cost? Does this service produce more (better) outcomes than the other service for the same money? A 'yes' to either of these questions means *this* service is more cost-effective than *the other*.

Figure 2.1 provides a visual representation of these decision rules. Findings can be 'plotted' on this graph using the vertical line to mark cost and the horizontal line to mark the effects. We return to this diagram in discussing the cost-effectiveness results in Chapters 5 and 6. The researchers in the Health Visiting and Adolescent Prevention studies estimated the cost of the additional outcomes that were produced by one of the services studied.[8] This 'incremental cost-effectiveness ratio' can then be compared with the results from other such studies as they occur.

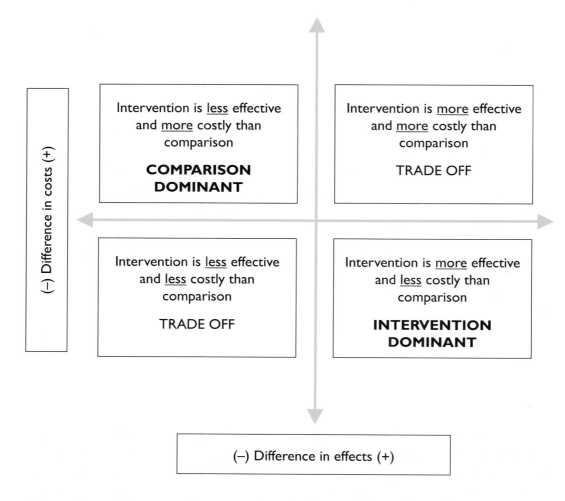

Figure 2.1 The cost-effectiveness plane (adapted from the Adolescent Prevention study)

The Health Visiting study was the only study to use techniques associated with cost-benefit analysis. A cost-benefit analysis often calculates the outcomes in money making a comparison of costs and outcomes easier. Researchers in this study surveyed parents of primary school children. They found that parents were willing to pay an additional average amount of £15 per day to reduce the chance of their

8   Change in outcomes from start of the 'intervention' to end of study
Change in support costs from the start of the 'intervention' to end of study

children being abused in a day nursery from 2 per cent to nothing. This provided an estimate of the *societal value of averting* the poor outcome. The figure can then be compared with the *costs of preventing* the same outcome to assess whether the amount spent on the intervention is cost-beneficial.

This initiative has far more to offer our understanding about the implications of spending money than the findings from formal economic evaluations. Some of the studies, quite rightly given their aims or the challenges of the research context, did not try to bring costs and outcomes together. Their focus was on estimating unit costs, usually for jointly provided services and support. The costs estimated in the Troubled Adolescents (3), Assessment Framework (6), and Child Protection (9) studies were, however, set clearly in the service context or in other literature on cost implications. They were also accompanied by information on children's or families' characteristics, needs and views.

Information on unit costs is useful in its own right (see Chapter 4). There is also a considerable amount to be learnt from the studies that use statistical analysis to explore why costs varied. Five studies used these techniques: Costs of Children in Need study (2), Therapeutic Family Support study (5), Care Leaver study (7), Children's Homes study (8) and Care Careers study (14). Using methods more commonly employed in other health and social care topics, these studies explored the links between costs and the characteristics and needs of the children (2, 8) and families they serve (5, 7), outcomes for the young people (5, 7, 8), or the characteristics of the services (5, 8, 14). The Adolescent Prevention and the Home-Start studies also used these techniques to help understand the findings from their comparative cost-effectiveness analysis.

Some studies moved away from these micro-level evaluations and took early steps into the broader field of child social care economics. The Foster Carer (10) and Adoption (13) studies looked at carer satisfaction and motivations and the role of financial incentives. Other studies explored the links between different parts of the care system (14) or agencies (3, 9). Regardless of any further statistical techniques used, these studies provide descriptive analytic information about how and why certain decisions are made and the implications of those decisions for the way resources are used.

The findings on costs and cost-effectiveness illustrate the possible impacts of decisions to spend money in particular ways. In this way they should be of great value to commissioners and managers. Care must be taken, however. The sources of uncertainty mentioned above are just as valid for cost-effectiveness findings as they are for assessing effectiveness. Moreover, there is no existing body of evidence on costs or economic evaluation of children's social care services. There is no history of prior research to help interpret the findings or with which the results can be compared. This means that if a study in this initiative found one way of doing something to be the more cost-effective option, we cannot be certain that is definitely the way forward. We return to these issues in Chapters 4, 5 and 6.

Conclusion

Decisions about how to spend money are continually taken and they can only be taken in an informed way if evidence on relative costs is available. Costs research is relevant because of its ability to stand outside any one organisation's or provider's viewpoint. It can take a broader perspective. It can look at costs by putting the child at the centre, just as would happen in children's outcome research. There are many different kinds of costs and research can supply information on what these costs are. The value of such research depends ultimately on the fact that there are not enough resources to meet all needs and demands. Choices have to be made, so to spend money on one service means that this money cannot be spent on another. For this reason the cost of a service has to be relevant to almost all the decisions that are taken about it.

The effects of a service are also clearly relevant to any decision to increase or decrease its volume. As we have seen it is hard to identify these effects. Any approach has drawbacks, so that it is only through the accumulation of research evidence that any high degree of certainty comes. And even if there is clarity about effects there may be uncertainty about how these are balanced. What is to be made of a service that is very popular with its users but does not appear to achieve the effects intended? Is a small increase on one measure worth the costs it has taken to achieve it?

Studies that assess both costs and effectiveness overcome some of these challenges. They are highly relevant to those who have to take decisions. Clearly the uncertainties pertaining to effectiveness research remain. So too do the ethical questions and political questions. For example, how should spending money on a cost-effective way of delivering residential care to adolescents be set against other ways of spending the money – for example, on transport, education or health? Theoretically it is possible to carry out research that will inform such broad debates. The research in this initiative has played a vital part of an ongoing effort where many challenges remain. For the moment those taking decisions in children's services have to rely on the best evidence available and thus on studies such as those summarised here.

Despite our emphasis on uncertainties, our overall message is a positive one. The studies we review have been well done. Much thought has been given to the best method of doing them. The results should be particularly relevant to the authorities that were prepared to be involved in them. (And for understandable reasons some were not.) In this way they should repay the altruism of the children, young people and parents who volunteered to take part in them. They did so in the hope that their views and experience would be of value on a much wider scale. We believe these hopes were well based. It is a challenge to all to ensure that they are fulfilled.

Summary

Actions based on research should be based on a clear understanding of the strength of the findings and the degree to which they are likely to apply in different contexts. For this reason it is important to understand how the research was done.

Studies in this initiative are among the first to estimate unit costs for children's social care services and social work processes, and to calculate the costs of care packages that cross usual service and agency boundaries. Many have been explicit about their approaches allowing them to be replicated.

Assessing effects is also complex. To link outcomes to services research must describe who will use the service, what the service provides, and what the service has achieved for its users. Each decision about assessments and analysis is underpinned by judgements and values and by ethical and practical constrains. Clarity about the research process can help, but researchers should be clear about the level of uncertainty surrounding the results.

To bring costs and effects together four main types of analysis can be identified from economic theory: cost-effectiveness, cost-utility, cost-consequences, and cost-benefit. Such studies look at the associations between spending money in particular ways and the impact on children and families. Studies in this initiative represent the some of the first steps in employing these types of analyses in the UK. The findings should help inform commissioners in their decisions about how to spend their limited resources.

Chapter 3

Delivering Care Services: The Ideal and the Reality

Introduction

How should social care services for children distribute their resources? What role is there for collaboration between different agencies? How far can there be a partnership between those using the services and those providing them?

Previous 'messages from research' overviews have been much concerned with these questions. Their descriptions of how services have been deployed in the past have helped create the new policy vision. They have also persistently pointed out that services fall short of the partnership ideal they propose. In this chapter we first describe this earlier work and then look at how far a similar critique might be applied to services available at the time of this initiative.

The conclusion of our historical review – and indeed the point of it – is that services have not moved much, if at all, in the direction implied by earlier critiques. The reasons for this have to be understood and addressed if the vision of a more preventive and integrated service is to be achieved.

Previous overviews: the ideal of partnership and prevention

Previous 'messages from research' overviews have fallen into two broad groups. First there have been overviews of the operation of social services with all or particular groups of children, for example, those in danger of abuse, teenagers, those at risk of entering the care system, those in need of support. Second, there have been studies of particular provisions: residential care, adoption and foster care (Department of Health 1998; Parker 1999; Sinclair 2005). In this chapter we will be concentrating on the first set of overviews since they lead us more naturally into a discussion of the way resources are distributed in relation to need.

Taken together these earlier studies have provided a surprisingly consistent line of argument. Briefly social services should, wherever possible, adopt approaches based on partnership and prevention. They should intervene before problems become entrenched, attend to the child's needs in the round and emphasise support as much as protection. In pursuing this wider remit they will need wherever possible to collaborate with others. In this way services will, as it were, work with the grain of the children's lives and that of their families.

The first two overviews, *Social Work Decisions in Child Care* (Department of Health 1985) and *Patterns and Outcomes in Child Placement* (Department of Health 1991), were concerned with the care system. The picture presented was a rather gloomy one. Thresholds of admission were high and decisions to admit were often made late and in a crisis. Social workers saw families not as allies but as adversaries whose importunate demands should be resisted or whose children should be forcibly removed. Families resented the refusal of requests for accommodation without the offer of alternatives, disagreed with the social workers over the use of control and resented the use of compulsory measures. The children and young people involved were described as poorly educated, relatively unhealthy, and liable to be precipitated at younger and younger ages into a world for which they were ill prepared.

The reports emphasised the key role of social workers in reversing this situation. If they were to become allies of families, they had to have the characteristics of accessibility, reliability, practicality and so on that the families valued. They had to become better informed about the families' difficulties and strengths and develop skills in working with them. To this end they should make greater use of day care and care by relatives. They should use short-term care to support families rather than supplant them, and ensure children did not drift in the care system. The social workers themselves required better and more frequent supervision, an effective policy framework and freedom from the less helpful features of bureaucracy.

A key feature of both reports was their insistence that social services departments should promote partnerships with other agencies and the children and their families. Partnerships with agencies would help them to respond better to the ordinary needs of children for good schooling and health care, and accommodation and financial support on leaving care. This would help them to build partnerships with children rather than just focusing on their status as children at risk or otherwise entitled to social services. For similar reasons social services needed to pay attention to contacts between families (including siblings and other relatives) and children 'in care'; to preventive work with families; to the use of relatives for foster care and to respite care. In the end all depended on the decisions and plans made for individual children. For this reason the skill of the social workers and in particular their ability to weigh and use evidence was crucial.

These first two overviews urged social workers to take a broad view of their clients' difficulties and wherever possible to work with families on them. The third report advocated extending this approach to children in need of protection

(Department of Health 1995). It pointed out that only around one in seven of those referred as children potentially at risk were actually registered as being so. Even fewer, around 1 in 25, were actually removed from home as a result. Thresholds for registration varied between authorities but in all authorities there was a tendency to concentrate on risk rather than need. A particular example of this tendency was the lack of provision for treatment even if the child was registered. Many children who were not registered as at risk were in considerable difficulty but often received little help.

In response to this situation the overview argued that the actual events that led to a referral were generally less important than their context – whether the child was being raised in a house low in warmth and high in criticism – and its outcome – whether in the long term the child's development was seriously harmed. In cases such as these, it was argued, it would have been better to concentrate on working with the family, defining the children as in need rather than as at risk, and on providing treatment and meeting needs.

The basic thrust of all three overviews was thus to emphasise the case for working with families in a way that was intended to keep children in their families and improve their outcomes. These outcomes were in turn conceived widely to include children's education, their emotional and physical well-being, their ties with their family and general sense of identity and their preparation for their future. In these ways the overviews both influenced and reflected the general climate of opinion that led to the Children Act 1989. They were also highly relevant to more recent initiatives, for example the promotion of the LAC recording system and the 'refocusing' debate, as well as the Quality Protects and Choice Protects initiatives.

Three subsequent 'messages from research' broadened and added detail to the general picture provided by the earlier ones: *Focus on Teenagers* (Department of Health 1996), *The Children Act Now* (Aldgate and Statham 2001), and *Supporting Parents* (Quinton 2004). The first of these called attention to the fact that teenagers could be children in need. Like the other reviews it argued for the need to meet service users halfway, and respond to their particular requirements and life-styles. It suggested that serious problems might be best met through 'multiplex' arrangements whereby different agencies combined to provide jointly planned accommodation and support.

The Children Act Now (Aldgate and Statham 2001) reviewed the progress in implementing the Children Act 1989. It reinforced the accounts of what families want from services, analysed what is meant by 'consulting with children' or 'partnership with families', and identified some of the steps that could be taken to make these a reality. It also noted a tendency in some authorities to restrict their definition of children in need to children at risk of abuse.

Recommendations from this overview called for improvements in inter-agency work, particularly between social services and health and education services, the development of a wide range of accessible and appropriate services, and the ability of social workers to work with families to use these resources appropriately. Whereas it pointed to good practice in all these respects it nevertheless felt that there was some way to go. This was particularly so in relation to inter-agency working where there was a lack of a common language for describing need along with a regrettable tendency for agencies to defend themselves against demand and pass the buck.

One of the most recent overviews, *Supporting Parents* (Quinton 2004), takes an even wider view of social services' potential clientele. This sees support as comprising a variety of different practical and emotional elements, which typically come from a variety of different sources. It suggests that most families want to organise their own support. They want support on their own terms and at times of their own choosing. They fear support that brings with it a loss of control over their own lives. It follows that support should be delivered in partnership with families and in the context of a relationship between the family and a trusted professional. In Chapter 5, we use the findings from one of the projects described in that overview.

Supporting Parents is even-handed in its appraisal of how far services correspond to this ideal. On the positive side it outlines the wide range of government initiatives designed to develop and co-ordinate support to families and emphasises the variety of measures, including financial, that contribute to support for families. Less positively the overview again comments that agencies fail to co-operate, offer support haphazardly, often defend themselves against demand, and deal in a partial way with particular problems. The reasons for these failures are seen as partly the perceived pressures on resources and partly the desire of professionals to defend their own territories.

Every Child Matters and previous research

Every Child Matters reinforces messages from research that have recurred since the mid 1980s. Researchers have repeatedly called on social services departments to view children's problems 'in the round', to intervene earlier and to collaborate better with other agencies. Despite official endorsement for these calls the picture of social services provided by studies in this initiative has changed little.

Two questions therefore arise:

- Why has so little changed?
- How far can new initiatives (Sure Start, Connexions and the like) substitute for the services traditionally provided by social services departments?

These three overviews set out a vision that is remarkably similar to that of the earlier 'messages from research' and also of current policies. The latter emphasise the need for services to work in collaboration with families and to be delivered in the ways that families find acceptable. It is expected that need will be widely defined and take account of children and their families' needs for education, health services, finance and information as well as social support. There will be a wide variety of services to meet these needs and they will be variously provided and co-ordinated by different agencies working together as well as by less formal groups. Social workers will retain a crucial role in working with families where risk is a genuine issue and by being experts at developing plans with families and the many agencies on whom they may call.

Every Child Matters is not the only government initiative to be informed by this vision. The desire for early intervention, 'joined up thinking' and collaborative approaches informs such major Government initiatives as Sure Start, the Connexions service, the Children Act of 2004, and the National Service Framework for Children, Young People and Maternity Services. There are related initiatives on information sharing and assessment, on the Integrated Children's System, and on a common framework for assessing children in need. Planning frameworks, service grants and guidance on procedures to be followed in cases of child abuse are all suffused with the ethos of collaboration. The ideas floated in the overviews are clearly ones whose time has come.

How far had these ideas informed practice at the time of the studies in the current initiative?

The current studies: the reality of resource distribution

Most of the studies summarised in this overview concentrated on children and young people in contact with social services. Although two studies focused on health providers and one included an educational service, the remainder were primarily concerned with clients using services either directly provided by social services or likely to be funded by them. It was thus striking that the studies' findings did not suggest that earlier interventions and supports were in place or that services were responding to a wide view of needs to the extent that the previous reviews have recommended. Instead the evidence suggested that at the time the studies were carried out:

- At any one time the numbers of children in need who are on the books of social services outnumber the total number of looked after children by a factor of more than six to one (2).[1]

- A very small proportion of those making an initial contact went on to receive a 'core assessment' (about 3% in study 6).

- Some of those whose cases were closed without a full assessment almost certainly had high needs (6).

- The level of apparent difficulties among service users in the community was very high, suggesting that the threshold for these services was also high (see, for example, studies 4, 5, 9, 13).

- Those receiving services generally appreciated them (1, 4, 5, 11, 14) but there was a more common view among the families that service provision was often 'too little too late' (4, 5, 13, 14).

- Where services were provided children and their families were often appreciative of the social workers (4, 5, 9), but some saw them as pre-occupied with risk at the expense of attention to the wider needs of the child (9).

- Removal to the care system or adoption was resisted, often until a late date, and to a point where the carers were desperate and the researchers felt that the child or young person was seriously damaged (4, 13, 14).

- Children who were looked after and who did not return home quickly tended to remain looked after until they 'aged out of the system', thus acquiring sustained attention over a long time (14).

- The children and young people who were subject to the most sustained attention did not necessarily receive a rounded service based on a wide assessment of their needs (13, 14).

In these ways social services departments have focused their attention on a small group of children who have severe difficulties, often of a kind that stigmatised either them or their families. Relatively few resources were devoted to early intervention. Nor was there much consideration of children's needs 'in the round'. Arguably other services such as health visiting or initiatives such as Sure Start meet the gap that social care services have left. As far as the services provided by social services departments are concerned, there is nothing in this description of the

---

1   The 2001 *Children in Need Survey* reported on more than 360,000 children who were 'on the books' of social services departments. Just fewer than 50,000 of these were reported as being looked after during the week of the survey. The number of children who come briefly on to the books of social services and then have their cases closed is almost certainly very large. The disparity between the numbers of children looked after at any point in a year and the numbers of children seen by social services during the whole year is almost certainly greater than one to six.

system that is incompatible with that provided in the earliest overview or, indeed, with that in any of the other overviews we have described. Why then has the vision of these overviews failed to come about? Has the argument in earlier overviews overlooked some fundamental difficulties concerned with implementing their recommendations? Can the research in these studies cast any light on what the difficulties might be?

The current studies: the reality of collaboration

If there were few resources devoted to early intervention were more devoted to those other imperatives of the new world: integration and collaboration? The researchers in this initiative certainly thought it should be. This was particularly so in relation to mental health, housing and education, although the focus of the collaboration varied with children's age and other characteristics. For example, there was a need to collaborate with housing and employment agencies on behalf of care leavers and with services for drug misuse for the families of some young children.

Despite these imperatives the evidence suggests that at the time the studies were carried out co-operation remained at best patchy. The Child Protection study (9) suggested that co-operation with mental health services was 'limited and fragmentary'. Thus:

- Use of child and adolescent mental health services was surprisingly low (4, 5, 13) despite evidence of very high levels of mental ill health among the children and care leavers (3, 4, 5, 7, 9, 13, 14).

- In general there was goodwill but there were said to be difficulties over lack of a common language, poor communication, different perceptions of client need and differences in power (9).

In general the researchers suggest that difficulties in co-operation can be overcome by such expedients as developing joint training and a common language of need. The researchers working on the Assessment Framework study, for example, suggested that collaboration would be promoted by greater clarity over the roles of different agencies, arrangements for sharing information, a common language, the Assessment Framework and opportunities for joint training.

Surprisingly the researchers made rather little reference to the effects of resources on collaboration. Resources, however, were obviously tight. This constrained practice. The Health Visiting study reported that health visitors regard 'ordinary' health visiting as 'crisis management'. Lack of time prevented them from practising as they wish. It seems possible that similar constraints prevented them from early intervention and from adopting the wide definition of need that co-operation requires.

Two studies are particularly relevant to this issue. These were the only ones that focused particularly on the links between agencies. The Child Protection study was concerned with links between social services and the child and adolescent mental health services (CAMHS), and the Troubled Adolescents study focused on links between social services and education.[2] Both studies pointed to substantial needs among social services clients that could, in theory, be met by the involvement of another service. Both also point to the substantial difficulties of achieving this.

Child Protection study (9)

The Child Protection study focused on 234 children from three local authorities, aged from 5 to 16 and subject to a recent child protection conference. Ninety-three per cent of the children appeared to have a recognisable psychiatric disorder.[3] Two thirds of them had siblings and around half had mothers who also had such problems. So there was a case for collaboration with adult services for those with addiction and mental health problems and an even more pressing case for collaboration with CAMH services over the children themselves.

Collaboration was constrained by numerous practical difficulties. The first of these concerned money. This was in short supply. In two of the three areas in the study CAMHS budgets were overspent. Financial considerations had an important impact on decisions. A CAMH service might deal with more than one local authority but not know how its services were distributed between them. Lack of money forces services to ration their resources and this in turn makes it harder for them to respond to requests from others.

The need to husband resources was apparent in a number of areas. Specialised referral routes (most referrals came via GPs rather than social workers), lack of key staff (one area lacked a child psychiatrist), problems of transport in rural areas and waiting lists all restricted demand. Waiting times to see a CAMHS worker varied from 12 to 25 weeks in one study area to a much longer six to nine months in another. The proportion of referrals to CAMHS from social services departments also varied between study areas – from 1.5 per cent to 16 per cent of the total. Even when contact was made it was rarely prolonged.[4]

---

2   Other studies (5, 8, 10) examined provisions in both social services and the independent private and voluntary sector. In these studies, however, the collaboration is rather different since, in many cases, the social services are paying for what is done and the work itself might be undertaken in either sector.

3   This figure refers to children whose files were judged to contain adequate information. It also depends on researcher judgements made from the files. Social workers completed a standardised mental health questionnaire for 99 children. This showed 40 per cent had scores at the clinically significant level. The actual figure is therefore subject to some doubt. What is not in doubt is that many of those named on child protection registers along with their parents have psychiatric disorders.

4   This finding is in keeping with another from the Adoption study. Only around one in six of the adopted children who had contact with CAMHS received more than an assessment (13).

Social services also had their difficulties. Out of the original five authorities one had 50 per cent of their current child protection workload unallocated, another was in special measures. Neither of these authorities took part in the phase of the study that explored the circumstances of children. The difficulties in the remaining authorities can be gauged from the problems they had in participating in the research. Despite being prepared to make up to four attempts, the researchers were not able to contact the relevant social workers for more than 102 out of 243 children in their sample. Social workers are likely to be the first port of call for workers in other services wishing to work with social services over particular cases. Their absence or low availability must make co-operation very difficult.[5]

Given the problems in both services it is not hard to see why, despite goodwill, co-operation was no more than patchy. Social workers seeking help for clients with mental health problems do not typically wish to wait nine months. By the time they have done so the situation may well have changed. Equally social workers may not find it easy to persuade families to attend for clinic appointments. In any event the chance of making a successful referral is almost certainly reduced if it has to go through two hands (first the GP and then the CAMHS practitioner). For their part hard pressed CAMHS staff may well find it difficult to adapt their service – for example, by making home visits, reducing waiting times and creating easier access. Demand for CAMHS currently outruns their ability to meet it. Why should they take on more and possibly less suitable clients?

Troubled Adolescents study (3)

This study focused on a sample from nine schools for children with Educational and Behavioural Difficulties (EBD schools), 11 children's homes and 138 foster care placements. The principal aims were to map the variations in users and organisational structures, to develop ways of estimating costs that could be compared, and to lay the ground for future research.

The study found considerable overlap in the needs of young people in EBD schools and the children's homes. Forty-one per cent of the children in children's homes and 49 per cent of those in EBD schools were said to have educational problems. The figures for emotional and personal problems were 68 per cent (EBD schools) and 64 per cent (children's homes). The figures for foster care were lower. However, the researchers also constructed a measure of 'adolescent difficulty'. On this measure they estimated that although proportionately English foster carers may look after fewer 'difficult' adolescents, the greater numbers in foster care mean

---

5   The national recruitment strategy for social workers is obviously seeking to address this problem, which is particularly acute in London.

that in total EBD schools, children's homes and foster carers may well be supporting similar numbers.

These similarities were accompanied by differences. Half the residents in children's homes had first separated from home when aged 12 or over. The comparable break point for foster care was eight years and three months, and it was nine years and eight months for EBD schools. Some of the reasons for separation were also different. Abuse, neglect and relationship problems at home were far more likely to be mentioned as reasons for leaving among the children's home and foster care samples.[6]

In comparison with children's homes, the EBD schools were larger, placed in rural rather than urban locations, generally longer established and better able to articulate their aims and methods. They were further from the young people's homes but generally operated a weekly boarding system, so that the pupils returned home at weekends. Half the schools kept the young people for four nights a week. Strikingly, all the children in the EBD sample but only half those in the children's homes were in full-time schooling, a finding that suggests there is much work for children's homes in this respect.

These differences were reinforced by some differences in values. Staff in children's homes seemed somewhat unaware of their residents' school activities and achievements. Staff in EBD schools had their own ethos that, according to the researchers, included a certain 'professional insularity'. Both sets of professionals sometimes had a limited knowledge of their residents' backgrounds.

So if children's homes and EBD schools have a similar clientele is there scope for them to act as complements or alternatives to each other? Would some young people now in children's homes do better in EBD schools with fostering in the holidays? Would the education of some of those in children's homes benefit from attending EBD schools on a day basis? And no doubt there are other possibilities. Local education policies on inclusive schooling obviously play a part in defining the availability and accessibility of such places but the researchers were concerned about the somewhat ad hoc use of placements in these two forms of provision. The new framework proposed in *Every Child Matters* suggests possibilities for a more systematic collection of statistics on EBD schools and for the development of a strategic approach at local level to cover both forms of provision.

In practice greater integration could well be difficult. A sizeable transfer of young people from one system to the other would also mean a transfer of costs.

---

6   This excludes those with short breaks. The histories were gathered from different sources (case files, EBD staff and residential staff) and the source may have influenced the likelihood that certain kinds of difficulty would be reported. However, differences in factual domains such as family structure suggest that the differences are probably real.

Funding streams for placements at these schools are already complex. The Troubled Adolescent study found they often involve complex negotiations between social services and the education authority, with the health sector increasingly becoming involved. At the same time those who now enter children's homes would need to be identified earlier or schools would have to admit older children.[7] The much higher prevalence of an abusive home environment among the residents of children's homes means that arrangements would have to be made to cater for young people who cannot go home at weekends and holidays, perhaps through the provision of foster care. There are already such arrangements but they would need to become much more frequent. Social care agencies would need to accept much about schools that they may currently find unacceptable, for example the rural location, the size of school and the sleeping arrangements.[8] Or the schools would need to change, which may mean they become more expensive. In many cases the concept of care would need to change. Social workers commonly hope against hope that time in the care system can be short, a breathing space or port in a storm. Schools by contrast are looking at an extended period of time over which change can be achieved.

These difficulties do not preclude the use of EBD schools for looked after children. They do, however, make it very difficult for children in the care system to access this service in large numbers.

Conclusion

Previous 'messages from research' have consistently argued that children's social care services should support a wide range of clients, adopt a wide definition of need, prevent difficulties as well as react to them, and operate in partnership with their clients and in close collaboration with other services. Over time these messages have been delivered in different ways not only through the previous overviews but also through the Children Act 1989, the refocusing debate, *Every Child Matters*, and the flurry of policy activity that accompanied the Children Act of 2004. The latter has required all agencies to work together to ensure availability of a range of preventive services. These are to be designed to meet needs at an early stage, and it is hoped will preclude the need for children to receive additional specialist and perhaps more costly services later.

---

7   Some of those in children's homes have entered the care system early. It is possible that they could be identified with some precision. Many, however, only start to get into difficulties relatively late. These children would be much harder to identify.

8   It should not be forgotten that social services presided over the demise of one school based system, the former Approved Schools (later CHEs). There is no research evidence on the effects of these two systems.

Issues for collaboration and early intervention

Over time services have adapted their provision to their clientele. Collaboration or changes in the way they target their services do not immediately create additional resources for these services, are likely to bring extra costs and may require them to offer a service they think less appropriate than their current one.

The kinds of change suggested by *Every Child Matters* are therefore likely to depend on:

- an ability to identify a high proportion of the children likely to have later problems
- an ability to 'screen out' children who are unlikely to have later problems
- putting in place interventions that are effective in preventing later problems
- a willingness to provide additional money to enable services to adapt and to serve children for whom early prevention is already too late.

Difficulties in meeting these conditions may account for the problems social services have had in responding to the calls from researchers and policy makers for greater collaboration and earlier intervention.

As we have seen the actual focus of social care services remains much more restricted than their potential remit might suggest. The research we have reviewed describes a fierce system of rationing, responses to a narrow definition of need and patchy co-operation with other agencies. Despite this context social workers often do create working alliances with their clients. Arguably, however, this has more to do with their dedication and skill than with the context in which they work. Why have the commissioners and main providers of care services for children tended to operate in this way?

The most obvious explanation is that resources are tight. Social services departments have always provided care away from home, often on a compulsory basis.[9] Twenty-four hour care cannot be provided 'on the cheap'. So a natural consequence of this responsibility is that the bulk of the resources of these departments have been devoted to the care system. Other resources are equally naturally spent on determining who can safely be left with no service or in monitoring those where

---

9   Historically children's departments grew up around the provision of foster care and residential care. Legislation after the war only gradually added in powers related to prevention.

there is continuing concern. The exercise of compulsion and the exclusion of less needy cases can both raise resentment and limit co-operation, a situation somewhat mitigated by the skill and dedication of staff and by the gratitude of those who receive support when and how they want it.

What implications might this have for the greater integration and more preventive approach envisaged in *Every Child Matters*? As we have seen something like it has been envisaged for a long time. The fact that it has not yet occurred suggests the extent of the challenges it poses. Why might this be so?

One reason may be that the savings that are supposed to follow from the preventive approach may not be large and will certainly not be immediate. The possibility of these savings depends on certain assumptions. These are:

- It is possible to identify those who would otherwise go on to develop the poor outcomes that render them liable to enter the care system.

- Those who are identified will wish to take part in the intervention.

- The intervention is effective.

- The intervention will not result in many more families receiving a costly service who would otherwise not have 'done badly' if left unsupported.

We will look later at some relevant results from these studies but at present there is little by way of conclusive evidence on the degree to which these requirements are met. What is clear from this chapter is that social services have tended to concentrate their efforts on cases that have passed the stage of early intervention. Work with young families with fewer difficulties today will not affect current teenage foster children who may once have been in such families. So any preventive effect of the new services will take a long time to work its way through the system.

Obviously, collaboration between practitioners will not in itself create additional resources and may be hampered by resource problems in the collaborating agencies. The processes of collaboration are not cost free; meetings and referrals take professional time.[10] Moreover the assumption behind collaboration is that services will meet a wider range of needs for the same people. So clients of social services may become more likely to be patients of CAMHS or pupils in receipt of educational psychology. Clearly it will not be easy to implement this programme as

---

10 Although the researchers were concerned about the quality of collaboration they recorded considerable efforts in pursuit of it. The Child Protection study estimated the time spent on various activities concerned with children who were the subject of a child protection conference. They estimated that social services staff spent on average 11.5 hours in meetings, 21 hours in telephone calls and 23.5 hours in recording on each case in a 9–12 month period. Both telephone calls and recording are relevant to collaboration and may be directly related to it. In contrast the social workers spent only 24 hours on visits.

well as one that promotes early intervention without the provision of more resources.

A rather different issue concerns organisational control and expertise. Previous overviews have complained that social services have defined their remit too narrowly. This has restricted their ability to attend to children in need and perhaps made them less ready to collaborate with other agencies over education or health. Less attention has been paid to its positive effects. A narrow remit provides an answer to the question of priorities. Faced with an array of needs they cannot fully meet social services have had to define priorities. The narrower the remit the easier this is to do. At the same time a relatively narrow remit makes it easier to define the expertise needed by staff and the role of managers in enabling the tasks to be done. Perhaps it is partly for these reasons that social services have moved away from the much more generic vision of social work implicit in the Seebohm (1968) report and the subsequent Barclay (1982) report.[11]

Similar considerations no doubt apply in other services. EBD schools receive their referrals from the school system, have teachers as the predominant professional group and are designed to address educational problems that affect a child's school life. They are not intended to supply a complete break from home. In all this they contrast with children's homes, which serve a clientele that is in certain respects similar. Any attempt to treat these schools as substitutes for or alternatives to children's homes would clearly require some considerable redesign.

None of these considerations imply that *Every Child Matters* is inappropriate. Collaboration does already happen. The Assessment Framework study suggests that initiatives which set a common framework of goals or which promote a common language or common referral protocols may well help it to happen more easily.[12] Multi-disciplinary teams should also make it less likely that families are passed from one agency to another. Local authorities take a quasi-parental responsibility for the children they look after so it is clearly essential that they attend to a wide range of their needs. Many families still complain of interventions that are too little and too late. There is an obvious case for responding to their needs as and when they occur.

---

11   As an example, many social services departments have chosen to pursue their priorities by creating specialist teams (such as teams for looked after children, disability teams and leaving care teams) rather than attempting to serve these groups through more generic teams, as was once the case.

12   At the same time it is worth noting that it is impossible to draw organisational lines in such a way that all forms of collaboration are encouraged. Social workers need to collaborate with schools and teachers. The new arrangements may make this easier. However, different structures may be required to encourage collaboration with other important services such as those concerned with poverty, domestic abuse and the abuse of drugs and alcohol.

It is also true that the new vision is for children's services as a whole. From a statutory point of view the new 'Social Care Services' will have a limited remit within a spectrum of services. The aim is both to prevent further Climbié tragedies and also to meet a far wider range of needs than has hitherto been the case. Social care services are concerned with the first part of this dual task. In pursuing this they need to ensure that those with whom they deal have a wide range of needs met. They are not responsible for the needs of all children. This change is a far cry from the universal ambitions of the Seebohm and Barclay reports, or even the expectations generated by the Children Act 1989 for dealing with 'Children in Need'.

That said, the facts remain that at present a very wide range of needs are not met; that meeting them will take resources; and that the challenges we have identified may well hamper the implementation of the new programme. So it is perhaps important for those responsible for this implementation:

- to be very cautious about assuming that early intervention will generate savings for the care system, or justifying it on that basis; it may be better to justify it on the basis of benefits to the recipients

- to have a keen eye for the costs of collaboration and attempt to provide it in the least costly way possible (for example, by exploring the degree to which consultation from clinical psychologists can act as an alternative to their direct intervention)

- to bear in mind the loss of organisational control and perhaps expertise that may come with broadening the remit of services.

If savings resulting from more preventative work, or indeed an injection of new funds, are not going to be forthcoming in the near future, then in the immediate future there may be a need to choose between providing support (spending money) on those currently in the care system or on the verge of it and increasing the amount spent on early intervention services. It will obviously be necessary to strike a balance. In doing this it is rational to examine how money is currently spent, what the costs are of providing the full range of supports in other ways and the effects of doing so. These are issues considered in the rest of the book.

Summary

Previous 'messages from research' have argued that social services should adopt approaches based on partnership and prevention. Today, the Children Act 2004 requires agencies to work together and to make available of a range of preventative services to meet needs at an early stage which may reduce the need for children to receive additional specialist and perhaps more costly services later.

As with the earlier research, the current studies suggest that earlier interventions or supports were not in place, and that services were not responding to a wide view of needs. Those receiving services generally appreciated them but the support was 'too little too late'. Resources continue to be focused on a small group of children with severe difficulties. Collaboration was patchy.

One reason that this long-existing policy agenda has not materialised in children's social services may be that resources are tight. Supporting children who cannot live at home is expensive, yet is an important part of social services agenda. Savings envisioned to come from preventative services will be slow to 'filter through' because spending on young children today cannot reduce overall spend on teenagers until those children reach their adolescent years – perhaps a decade hence. Collaboration has the potential to help to meet children's needs but can be costly in staff time. It may also increase demand on children's services as a wider range of needs is identified.

Directors of children's services therefore must make choices about how to spend their budgets; how to strike a balance between providing for those currently in the care system or on the verge of it and a range of earlier interventions. Information on how money is currently spent and to what effect should form an important part of their knowledge base.

Chapter 4

Costs and the Way they Vary

Introduction

One of the dilemmas facing the new directors of children's services is how they should spend social care resources to improve outcomes for some of the most vulnerable children in society. As we pointed out in Chapter 1, knowing how money is spent today can help decisions about how to spend it in the future. Does the current pattern fit expectations and plans? Should expenditure patterns continue in the same way or change?

What types of information do these studies provide that might help commissioners and managers make decisions about expenditure? This chapter considers three sets of information. We look at some of the new areas of unit costs that have been estimated in these studies and how these are used to calculate 'care package' costs. The focus is on the way children and young people use services, rather than the way social care services are provided. We also look at 'hidden costs', that is support costs that social care services may not see because another organisation funds them. Finally we look at why the costs of supporting children and young people differ. This type of information will help planners link their available resources with population needs.

We repeat an important point. This research initiative is called Costs *and* Effectiveness of Services to Children in Need. It advocated collaboration between researchers with economic *and* child care perspectives. Although this chapter is mainly about costs the information should always be read in the context of children's needs and outcomes. With today's constrained budgets it is difficult to operate without considering costs but it would be irresponsible to consider costs separately from the needs of children and their families.

Figure 4.1 shows a common view of how money in children's social care services is spent. It is taken from social services' financial returns to central government and shows the proportion of expenditure on broad service categories. In this chapter we take a different view and look at how money is spent on children. Chapter 1 described this approach. Children often use several different services so the costs of supporting one child will cross the service categories shown in Figure 4.1. Looked after children may be placed in foster care but they will also be supported by a social worker. Children living with their families might see a social worker, use a family centre and a grant might be provided to help with a particular expense. How can these 'support package' costs be estimated?

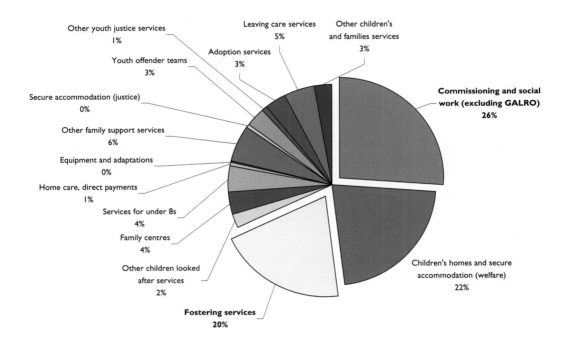

Figure 4.1 PSS expenditure on children's services 2003–4 (Data source: Department of Health 2005)

Calculating support package costs

The costs of a child's support package can be estimated as

- the number of contacts with each service over a given period

  multiplied by

- the time taken for each contact

  multiplied by

- the unit cost of each service.

Two pieces of information are central to this calculation. First, how much of any given service does this child use? None of the studies found enough information in case files on the way services are used. In many cases, placement histories were incomplete, records of the time spent by social workers were missing and meeting participants were not recorded. Where service use was recorded, it usually only related to social care services. Information on education attendance, use of health or youth justice services made only a rare appearance. Referrals to another service might be recorded, but not whether that service was actually used. Studies wanting this more 'comprehensive' view of service use collected the data from the children and families themselves.

The second piece of information needed is a unit cost for each service that the child or young person has used (see Chapter 2). There is no doubt that this initiative has made a vital contribution to knowledge about the unit costs of children's social care services. Alongside unit costs of more standard services such as children's homes, or EBD schools (see Box 4.1), three developments are particularly important. First some studies have estimated unit costs for *social work processes*; for example, in the Assessment Framework, Adoption and Care Careers studies (see Boxes 4.2, 4.3 and 4.4). These provide a more detailed look at that 26 per cent of social services money that is spent on 'commissioning and social work'.

Box 4.1 Residential care

Children's Home study (2001–2)
Excluding in-house education
30 LA residential homes:
     mean £1491 per resident week

15 P&V homes:
     mean £1664 per resident week

All homes
Including in-house education if provided:
     £622 to £3823 per resident week

Costs of Children in Need study (2000–1)
1115 residential placements
     mean £1300 per resident week
     median £1155 per resident week

Troubled Adolescents study (2000–1)
6 residential homes (excluding education):
     £1185 to £1820 per resident week

7 EBD residential schools:
     £600 to £1490 per resident week

Box 4.2 Assessment Framework study (2000–1)

For a core assessment:

Time sheets from 17 social workers from 4 local authorities verified by consultation; 26.25 social work hours over several weeks.

£657 for the social worker's time, £63 for other social services' colleagues, £133 for colleagues in other agencies.

Box 4.3 Adoption study (2000–1)

Costs for social work processes were estimated as:

£12,075 per child for placing a looked after child for adoption (96 children)

£6070 per child per year for maintaining a looked after child in an adoptive placement before making an adoption order (96 children)

£2334 per child per year for providing adoption support services to adoptive families post-Adoption Order (64 children).

Box 4.4 Care Careers study (2001–2)

Social work processes for looked after children

Standard costs to social services for eight social work processes identified from the Core Information Requirements.

Deciding child needs to be looked after	£508
Care planning	£95
Maintaining the placement	£1343 per month, includes placement cost
Leaving care/accommodation	£209
Finding a subsequent placement	£163
Review	£324
Legal interventions	£2198 (for making a care order)
Transition to leaving care services	£925

The second development occurred in the Therapeutic Family Support study, which described and costed the various supports that can be provided under a single roof (see Box 4.5). Easily accessible, multi-function services are becoming more common. Commissioners and managers need to know how the budget relates to the interventions and supports that are provided within such services to assess what needs are being met and at what cost.

Box 4.5 Therapeutic Family Support study (2000–1)

Average costs per session:

- £52 for one-to-one counselling
- £80 for family therapy
- £32 for early years/educational interventions
- £31 for parenting skills interventions.
- £32 for group work
- £34 for practical interventions.

The final set of new unit cost estimations looked at different ways of providing a similar service. For example, three studies compared services provided by local authorities and the independent sector: the Therapeutic Family Support, Children's Homes and Foster Carer studies. For residential and foster care, a tentative conclusion would be that although with a simple comparison of costs the independent sector may appear to have higher costs per week[1] a closer look shows that these services often include a wider range of supports – perhaps for carers or to meet children's education or mental health needs.

As a final note on unit costs we can look at the costs of collaboration. For example, assessment and other meetings should include representatives from other agencies to work together to a common end for children. But attendance at meetings, or even liaison, can be as costly for these agencies as for social services. The unit costs estimated in the Child Protection and Care Careers studies showed that at least a third of the total costs of meetings and other liaison activities might be borne by other agencies (see Box 4.6). The Assessment Framework study found

---

1   The Children's Homes study found that, after allowing for the cost of education, homes in the independent sector were not significantly more expensive than local authority ones.

this investment of inter-agency resources does appear to be paying dividends. The Child Protection study found closer collaboration between services also brought better knowledge about what each service does and may discourage one set of services from seeing another as a 'free' resource. It may also mean that a service beneficial to all collaborators is identified. Jointly provided and jointly funded services, such as some of the Home-Start projects, have the advantage of bringing together small amounts of money from several agencies. Given that all agencies have limited and constrained resources available, it might be easier for them to find these smaller amounts of money than to fund a whole new service.

Box 4.6 Child Protection study (2002–3)

Collaboration costs are estimated as:

Initial child protection conference: £304 excluding travel and preparation time
Social services 26%, health 34%, education 17%, police 9%.

Child protection review conference: £224 excluding travel and preparation time
Social services 23%, health 38%, education 20%, police 3%.

How social services spend their money on children

Even the quickest glance at Figure 4.1 will show that over 40 per cent of social services' expenditure is on placements for looked after children. In 1994–5, 15 per cent of social services expenditure was for foster placements and 27 per cent for children's homes. Although the proportion of expenditure on each of the two placement categories has changed over the past ten years, the total remains at around 42 per cent. Despite providing a range of services for children in different circumstances, there is a clear and long-standing trend for social services to spend a high proportion of their budgets on the smaller looked after population.

This may be a perfectly reasonable way forward. It suggests that social services target their resources on those most in need. Given that policy has for some time encouraged maintaining children in their own homes, the logical corollary is that if children are accommodated away from home they have much greater support needs that those who can stay at home. This uses a very broad definition of needs, but on the whole greater needs imply receipt of more intensive, therefore more costly, support.

The national Children in Need Services and Expenditure Survey (CIN) (DfES 2003) took a new approach to counting money. It focused on the costs of all social services' supports used by children rather than as absorbed by the services provided. So the total costs *per child* include what that child has received by way of payments for placements, one-off payments as well as the costs of group work and individual work from social workers and other care staff.[2] So, for example, it was possible to see how much of the expenditure on 'commissioning and social work' shown in Figure 4.1 was spent on children who also had money spent on them from the 'children's homes' or 'fostering services' segments.

Around 60 per cent of cases 'on the books of social services' had received support in the CIN survey week. Researchers in the Costs of Children in Need study carefully checked the 2001 cost and service use data.[3]

- For children receiving support in the survey week, at a mean cost per child per week of £450 (median = £273), looked after children were around four times as costly as children supported in their families or independently (mean = £110 per child per week, median = £51).

- These are average costs for care packages provided by social services to 50,000 looked after children and just over two-and-a-half times as many – 128,000 – supported children.

- Around two-thirds of total social services expenditure on children in need was spent on looked after children.

Mean and median costs

Mean costs are more useful for planning purposes as they take account of children who have exceptionally high (or low) costs.

The median is the cost of supporting a 'typical' child and is useful to planners where costs will not vary very much.

Commonly in health and social care services, median costs are less than mean costs. This implies there are a few high cost children. The larger the difference between mean and median costs, the greater the variability.

---

2   The accommodation category includes care while placed for adoption, foster placements, residential home placements, adoption allowances, residence order payments, Section 17 payments, Section 24 payments, and other ongoing payments. Not surprisingly, given the complexity of the task, most activity and cost errors were for centres or teams that provided both group and individual work.

3   Children with 'improbable or suspect' costs (say, a unit cost of less than £1 per day for residential care) were excluded from the analyses leaving a sub-sample of 177,570 of the children who received services in the CIN survey week. This sub-sample was the same as the full group of 241,598 children receiving services in terms of age, gender, population using each service etc.

This 'snapshot' survey emphasises the skew in expenditure towards looked after children referred to in the previous chapter. In the first place, the 42 per cent of expenditure spent on residential care and foster placements shown in Figure 4.1 rises to about 65 per cent when the relevant parts of the other service categories (segments) are included. Second, there were around 40 per cent of children 'on the books' who were not seen in the survey week and would appear as having no social services' resources spent on them. These children are most likely to be living with their families but they may still have high levels of needs.

There is no reason to assume that the CIN survey week was different from any other week in social services. In any given week, some children will have been in contact with social services for many months or years and some will have just been referred.[4] In any given week some children 'on the books' will receive a service and some will not, although it is likely that money will be spent every week on almost all looked after children.[5] However, what such 'snapshot' surveys cannot show is whether there is a change in the level of activity during the year. There may be higher numbers of children receiving support during other weeks of the year. Alongside accounting differences, this may account for slightly lower expenditure showed by CIN 2001 (about 15% when converted to a yearly amount) compared to the PSS expenditure returns.

Hidden costs

As well as providing social care services, social services departments have had to ensure children's needs 'in the round' are met, in particular aiming to improve their educational and health outcomes. We should, therefore, expect that children supported by social services will use schools and other education support, and may, for example, see a general practitioner. They might also be in contact with the youth justice system or use hospital or mental health services. Thus part of the cost of a child's 'support package' is borne by other organisations and services. These costs are often 'hidden' from social care managers' view because they come from another organisation's budget.[6]

---

4 Of those who received support, nearly two-thirds had been known to social service for more than six months. 20,588 children had been referred during the survey week (8,450 on the first day). The researchers had some concerns about the accuracy of the referral date given that just 7,330 children had been referred in the week prior to the survey.

5 In the week of the CIN 2001 survey, 10 per cent of children looked after and just under a half of all children supported in their families received no support. Twenty-two per cent of children named on the Child Protection Register received no support.

6 A common resource for unit costs was *The Unit Costs of Health and Social Care*. This is an annual volume published by the PSSRU at the University of Kent, Canterbury (www.pssru.ac.uk).

In the world of integration and collaboration proposed by *Every Child Matters* many such services and costs will come under the responsibility of the Directorate of Children's Services. So for children and young people using social care services, what are the costs of support provided by these other services and organisations?

- The non-social services costs of residential care are between 6 per cent and 10 per cent of the total cost of residents' care packages (studies 3, 8, 14).

- Family support services can generally be provided at a relatively low cost yet their users often have multiple problems. The costs of social care services absorbed around half of users' total support package costs, with the therapeutic family support services accounting for less than 10 per cent. Thus, nearly half the total support costs for these families in need were borne by health and education services.

- Social services funds only about a third of the total costs of care packages for young people supported by specialist adolescent support teams. In turn, less than a quarter of this was for direct support from the adolescent support teams.

It is not only services that bear these 'hidden' costs. Home-Start recruits and manages volunteers who provide support in young families' homes. The costs of volunteers are excluded from funding bids and contracts and therefore hidden from social services' view. The costs are, however, very clear to the volunteers who choose to give up their time to provide support. Were volunteers not available the costs of this service would rise with the necessity to pay the home visitors.

The Foster Carer study took place in the context of debates about the level of payments to foster carers and highlights concerns about families' additional costs in supporting looked after children. The Adoption study found similar concerns. Only about a third of adoptive parents in this study received adoption allowances but on average they spent around £2200 over and above normal childcare expenses. A fifth of adoptive families had purchased private sector health, therapy or education services. Many families had exhausted their savings. In the most recent year of adoption, a third of adoptive mothers and a tenth of adoptive fathers had still been unable to return to work or had to adapt their work patterns to care for their child.

Social care services make choices about how to support a child. These choices have an impact on their budget but also on the budgets of other agencies. In the case of residential care, where shelter, food and formal care (instead of informal care through parenting) are provided on one site, the impact on other budgets is small. Although the *absolute* costs are lower for young people using the adolescent support teams, where residential care is more often avoided, families bear a greater proportion, mainly in providing shelter, food, etc. However, in the case of adoption, families also pay for many direct 'treatment' costs.

These findings raise three issues for social care services. First, given that placements and other social care services absorb nearly all the costs of supporting looked after children are these services also meeting almost all their needs? If not, are there better ways of spending those same resources to meet residents' needs? Second, and relevant for both foster and adoptive carers, how much support for these vulnerable children should be funded by their carers? Third, a much smaller proportion of the total costs of supporting children who are not looked after is funded by social services; what influence should we expect these services to have on users' outcomes and how can this best be measured? We return to some of these issues in subsequent chapters.

Why the costs of supporting children vary

We should expect the costs of supporting children who use social care services to vary. If someone has broken a bone in their leg we would expect them to receive very similar treatment as others with a broken leg. So the costs will be very similar for everyone treated for a broken leg. Social care services are far more complex than those required to fix a broken leg. Children and young people's difficulties vary and range across many aspects of their lives, their family environments are different, their needs are different – the list goes on. So we should expect them to receive different services and different amounts of each service. In turn, this will mean different support package costs.

Is there any pattern to this variation in costs? Box 4.7 summarises some of the reasons why costs might vary but little is known about the way such factors influence the costs of child social care or the costs of support packages for children and young people. We note some of the studies from this initiative that start to look at these issues. Across the initiative, are there any characteristics, difficulties or needs that consistently raise or lower the costs of support? Knowledge of these, alongside similar information about their population would allow social care services to 'predict' the resources they might require if the service mix were to remain the same.

Variations in the costs of social care services

Four studies measured only the costs to social care services, including the Costs of Children in Need study. Secondary analysis of the Children in Need survey showed that children supported in their families had higher support costs where they lived in a London authority, belonged to a low-income family or had absent parents, where the children were older or babies, and if they were named on the Child Protection Register, receiving post adoption support or seeking asylum. Children who were disabled had lower support costs than non-disabled children.

For looked after children in the CIN 2001 survey, some of these 'cost drivers' were similar. Costs were higher for children supported by a London (UK) borough, if they had socially unacceptable behaviour, or if they were older children or babies. Costs were also higher if children were named on the Child Protection Register, receiving post-adoption support, or were seeking asylum.

Box 4.7 Reasons for cost variation

Over and above different ways of estimating costs, perhaps due to different accounting conventions or the scope of inputs included, there are eight main reasons why costs might vary.

1 *Resource prices (supply) and fiscal pressure*
   This refers to the amounts social services must pay for service inputs such as staffing. Some 'less desirable' localities offer a higher scale point, for example, or pressure on resources may mean lower prices are paid (see for example studies 2, 10, 14).

2 *Service outputs*
   What the service does, perhaps the number of places, whether a residential home has a school attached, or whether specific interventions are provided in a family centre (see for example studies 3, 5, 8).

3 *User characteristics and needs (demand)*
   These might be the age or gender of the children served, or the type or severity of the problems faced by themselves or their families (see for example studies 2, 7, 8, 11, 13, 14).

4 *User outcomes*
   Whether there is any change in child or family well-being (see for example studies 1, 4, 8, 11, 12, 13).

5 *Rate of service delivery*
   Occupancy rates or throughput of cases are examples here (see for example studies 2, 8, 10, 14).

6 *Management sector*
   Whether the service is provided within the public sector (NHS Trusts or social services, for example) or by for-profit or non-profit organisations (see for example studies 3, 5, 8, 9, 10, 11).

7 *Quality of care environment*
   Examples might be the design or upkeep of the building, management style, different types of therapies available, or whether there are clearly stated aims for the service (see for example studies 1, 3, 5, 6, 7, 8, 14).

8 *Geographic location*
   Costs for services in London are known to be considerably higher than the rest of the UK. There are other smaller regional differences. For the most part these variations are due to differences in resource prices (see for example studies 2, 8, 9, 10, 14).

Researchers on the Care Careers study took a different approach. The overall aims of this study were to explore the associations between costs and the care provided for looked after children, and to devise methods for local authorities to calculate the cost implications of different types of placements and for children with different needs. Data were collected from management information systems and case files on the background, needs and experiences over 20 months of a specially selected sample of 478 young people aged 11–17.[7] Unit costs for eight social work processes for looked after children were estimated (see Box 4.4). The researchers then developed a computerised system, the Cost Calculator, to perform the cost calculations that related the data on children to the unit costs enabling them to track the sequential costs incurred over specific time periods.

The researchers identified eleven groups of children:

- 129 children with no additional support needs

- 215 children who were allocated to four 'simple' groups where the child had: a physical or learning disability; an emotional and behavioural disorder; showed offending behaviour; or was an unaccompanied asylum-seeking child. There were between 10 and 129 in each of these groups.

- The remaining children (n=134) were divided into six 'complex' groups with between 1 and 72 in each group. These children had either two or three of the additional support needs identified in the four simple groups.

Costs per annum rose with the increasing complexity of children's support needs. For those with no additional support needs, the average cost to social services was £27,000 per annum. For those children with an emotional or behavioural problem (n=129), who had offended (n=46), or who were unaccompanied asylum seekers (n=109), the yearly costs were £41–45,000 per child. Costs rose for children with disabilities (£62,000 per annum, n=30) and were much higher for children in the complex groups. Social services' costs for the 46 children with disabilities and emotional and behaviour problems were £76,000 per year, and £79,000 per year for the 72 children who had emotional and behavioural problems and had offended.

This 'cost gradient' is not surprising and many authorities are currently looking at the children in their highest cost placements to see if the money could be spent more wisely. The strength of the Cost Calculator lies in the way that costs over time

---

7   The aim was to obtain a sample of 40 children in residential care, 30 in foster care (of whom 10 were living in kinship placements), and 20 children living at home or independently in each authority. The final sample of 478 young people excluded those using short-break (respite) care. One of the criteria for selection of the local authorities was that it had at least 30 children in residential care.

can be tracked for children alongside information on their needs and characteristics.[8] It allows commissioners to see how money and social work services were used to support particular groups of children, and gives them the potential to extrapolate these data into the next financial year(s). It can also help identify the short- and medium-term cost implications of social work decisions; perhaps about the type of placement selected, or the costs of a sequence of placements that break down or the implications of a distant placement for social work costs. These all add to an understanding of how money spent in one 'segment' of Figure 4.1 has implications for another.

Some social work decisions will lead to costly solutions. For example, an out-of-area placement may appear an expensive choice. But it may also be the appropriate place for a child whose high support needs cannot be met any other way. Both the Adoption and Care Careers studies showed how unstable care careers, often due to high needs and very challenging behaviours, can result in frequent changes of high cost placements leading to rising costs over time. High needs and challenging behaviour do not have to result in unstable care careers. An unstable care career may simply mean that services are failing the child. Both these studies suggest that higher investment in appropriate supports at earlier points in the child's care career may have been a wise investment. The Adoption study found that having clear plans based on assessment was important. The Care Careers study pointed to other organisational features that appear to raise social services' support costs for looked after children; lack of placement choice (leading to high use of agency or out-of-area placements), high use of temporary placements, extensive use of agency staff and some placement allocation procedures.

Consideration of organisational issues leads to analyses of the differences between authorities. Two studies undertook this type of work by looking at routinely collected measures.

The Foster Carer study explored the relationship between foster carer expenditure (20% of social services expenditure, Figure 4.1) and a number of performance indicators, including the proportion of looked after children in foster care.[9] The findings showed that, relatively speaking, the higher the number of children who are looked after, the lower the proportion of looked after children in foster care. But this association is only apparent if account is taken of how local authorities chose to spend their money. Higher gross spend per 1000 children and families, higher proportions of money spent on foster care services and on children in need and lower

8   The Cost Calculator has since been piloted and is being developed as a practical tool for use by social care agencies.

9   Also the A1 PAF indicator (the proportion of children looked after at 31 March who have had three or more placements) and the D35 indicator (the proportion of those looked after continuously for four or more years on 31 March who have been in the same foster placement for the past two years). Both these exclude children looked after on an agreed series of short-term breaks.

weekly costs per child were all associated with higher rates of foster care. All these factors played a part in 'explaining' the difference in rates of children looked after in foster care.

Individually, none of these findings come as a surprise. A commonly heard argument is that the more children requiring looked after services, the harder it is for local authorities to find enough foster care placements. The interplay of these factors suggests that a change in this performance indicator requires concerted action between those placing children, those recruiting and supporting carers, and those responsible for the way money is spent.

The Costs of Children in Need study also looked at differences between authorities. Earlier in this chapter we reported the *between-child* cost variations. Here the aim is to explain the differences in the *average* cost per authority. Average costs per authority for looked after children and for children supported in their families were explored separately. Even after taking into account the different populations served by each authority[10] there were still large cost differences between authorities for both groups of children. But factors outside the control of local authorities had only a small additional impact on these average costs. The number of children in need relative to the population slightly reduced the cost (for supported children only), relatively higher labour prices were associated with higher costs, and authorities with larger populations may have advantages in economies of scale. There was only a slight indication that if budgets were higher – other things being equal – expenditure per child is higher. Notably, management and social work staffing levels were not associated with average spend per child, neither were the children services' performance indicators, nor the relative proportions of looked after and supported children.

Variations in the public sector costs of support

Four studies looked at cost variations using a wider perspective than just costs to social services. They included supports provided by education, health and mental health services, and youth justice.

The Therapeutic Family Support study found higher costs were associated with children who had cost more to support before using the family support services, or had a qualified social worker as key-worker. These are service-related measures that may also indicate higher needs. Older children and those who used a voluntary sector centre were also more costly to support.

---

10   Characteristics of the children (such as age, needs, whether disabled, etc.) accounted for only an eighth of the variation in the *average* cost per child per local authority.

The Home-Start study found support costs were higher for families who had more children with special needs and where mothers' had higher levels of depressive symptoms. Higher parental distress scores were associated with lower costs but also strongly correlated with depressive symptoms so it was difficult to disentangle the two influences. The age of the oldest child was also positively associated with costs. Once these baseline characteristics had been taken into account, being in receipt of Home-Start and having lower household income increased costs and use of community support groups reduced costs.

Higher costs for young people using adolescent support teams were found for young people with a disability, who had ever been in care, or who did not live with at least one birth parent and with higher costs of care prior to entering the study.

Higher costs for young people using leaving care services were found for young people who had more placement moves, or for whom family support was perceived to be weaker, or who had mental health or emotional and behavioural problems. There was also weak statistical evidence to suggest lower costs were associated with disability but when support costs excluding accommodation were compared the small number of disabled young people were found to receive more costly support that their non-disabled peers.

Summarising cost variations

On the one hand these findings on why costs vary are quite encouraging. They suggest that people with higher needs in some domains are getting higher cost support packages relative to those with lower needs. Thus there appears to be some targeting of social care and other services' resources. Some needs are fairly consistently associated with higher costs: disability, absent or poor home environment, emotional and behavioural problems, mental health problems or socially unacceptable behaviour. The child's age and their previous care history also appear to have an influence, although not always raising costs.

That the 'predictor' variables are not always the same is in part to do with the different aims and clienteles of the services, and in part to do with the different measures the studies used. More consistent measures on needs and information about *severity* of, say, disability or emotional and behavioural problems, and better recording of service use may strengthen the predictive capacity of such analyses. These pieces of information might also be helpful to practitioners trying to set up a package of support to meet assessed needs.

It was striking that in all these studies the proportion of variation in costs that could be explained was not high: about a third for the CIN 2001 data and usually less than a fifth in the studies with smaller samples. While no one would want to see regimented child social care services in which all children received exactly the same set of supports regardless of their need, this does imply that social services have been using their resources in very different ways. Given that some ways are presumably 'better' than others there must also be much room for improvement.

Conclusion

This chapter focuses on the cost of the combinations of services children and young people receive alongside their characteristics and needs. Some studies focus on social care services and costs. Others take a wider view that is more in line with requirements for integration and collaboration of front-line services. They consider service use and costs across a wider range of agencies: education, health and the criminal justice system as well as social care.

Recording service use

One difficulty highlighted in many studies that has implications for integrated working, was that use of services was not routinely recorded in social services' case files or management information systems. While it may be easier to understand the absence of information about use of services provided by other agencies, it is less easy to see why such data about service use within social services are so often missing. Of course, such data are not necessarily better recorded in other agencies' case files but the development of routine recording systems will be crucial as services work towards greater integration.

If cross-agency service use data were recorded, it would be easier to see where there are gaps in a child's support package vis-à-vis their needs assessment – perhaps a referral that has not resulted in the service being used. There might also be overlaps, where two agencies unknowingly provide similar services – perhaps respite care in a hospital as well as in a children's home. Being able to see service responses 'in the round' may also throw into sharp relief how decisions taken by one part of the service, or in one provider agency, have had consequences for others.

The Care Careers study researchers commented, 'that such data are largely inaccessible should be addressed in implementing the Integrated Children's System'. Although integration in services, in support packages, and in information systems is the ideal, it may take a while to implement fully. Data flows that operate across service and agency boundaries may take even longer and may fall foul of data protection legislation or user preferences on confidentiality. Researchers in these studies generally found that young people and their parents/carers were able to report what services they had used recently. There is good research evidence from other fields to suggest that: they can remember *what* services they used; that their recall spans the full spectrum of services available; their memory of the frequency of service use compares reasonably well with case records (where this can be tested), particularly for shorter periods; and their memory of the length of time a service was used compares well with case records where it has had a big impact on their lives (for example, a stay in hospital or other location away from home) and for services that happen fairly regularly. This suggests that social workers could glean good quality information about a young person's care package just by asking that person or their carers without recourse to formal – but still developing – information sharing arrangements.

Unit costs

Underpinning the calculations of support package costs is the work done on unit cost estimations. This activity requires a clear description of each service. If such descriptions were more widely available it might also allow social workers to make a closer fit between children's needs and what supports the service may be able to provide.

These descriptions underpin unit cost estimations. Just as each service comprises different staff mixes and levels or has different outputs (overnight stays, number of therapy sessions, etc.) so too will unit costs be different. Average costs for a broad group of services can be misleading. Several studies in this initiative found considerable variation in costs between, say, all children's homes, or between social work teams that have a different purpose. These studies also provide some of the first information on the cost implications of how social workers spend their time, perhaps in assessment or review meetings.

Costs variation

Variation should be of real interest when looking at costs. Indeed, we should expect cost variation. Costs will vary for a whole range of reasons that can be measured at the child-level, perhaps their age or their level of difficulties as well as their outcomes. But they can also be a consequence of broader factors such as the different balance of care services in any area (say, relative numbers of places in foster care and children's homes or the level of provision of earlier intervention services), the quality of that care, or the geographical location of the authority or service (London prices tend to be higher than other areas of the UK). These studies start to address reasons for cost variation. The findings suggest there is much more to discover. More than two-thirds of the cost variation between children could not be explained. What choices are local authorities making about how they spend money that have not been captured by these studies? Are some of these choices 'better' than others?

Responding to the new policy environment

Social services clearly spend a high proportion of the resources at their disposal on looked after children. One the one hand, this is a rational choice about spending most money where there is greatest need. On the other hand the policy requirement is to change the balance of care – to provide more early interventions and preventative services.

One of the underlying aspirations of the new children's service policies is that supporting children and parents earlier in their 'service career' will improve short-term outcomes. In turn, this may also help avert poor outcomes in the future. A consequence of this would be reductions in the future spend on 'later interventions'. Changing the balance of care to achieve this is likely to happen over quite a lengthy period of time. After all, it has taken some 40 years to change the balance of care in the mental health system from one based on long-stay psychiatric hospitals to a more community-orientated system – and there is still much progress to be made.

So the dilemma for directors is to find out how, why and to what effect children's social care resources are currently deployed – and findings from this initiative can certainly help in that respect. They must then decide whether this is the pattern required or wanted in the future. If a change in the overall distribution is required there are two main routes: funding for 'double-running' costs or a fairly immediate reduction in one part to increase another part's share. Double-running costs may be required because the need for high cost 'later interventions' will only reduce gradually – and will probably not disappear completely – so money must be spent on these services. At the same time, providing more preventative services will absorb more resources. Any impact preventative services may have will take time to work its way though the age groups and then through to the care system, so savings here will not occur quickly. Central government initiatives over the last five to ten years, such as Sure Start, have been trying to support this process. But as Chapter 3 showed, their effect to date has been limited and as some of the studies in this research initiative show they may also have a case finding role – increasing demand for social care services in the short term.

The second way of achieving such a change in the balance of care is to shift resources within children's social care services from some of the 'segments' shown in Figure 4.1 to others. At the macro-level this appears a sensible solution given that budgets for children's services are constrained. (Scarcity of resources mean central government must make decisions about how much money to allocate to social services as well as to, say, the health service, or the armed forces.) One way of achieving this might be to slice a relatively small proportion of money from a high cost part of the children's services system to give a relatively large boost to lower cost parts.

Residential care is probably the most expensive care option; even a low cost residential placement may cost social care services ten times more than the cost of supporting a young person through an adolescent support team. In theory, this would mean that for the cost of one young person's residential placement, that young person and nine others could be supported in the community. However, to 'break even' we would have to be *very* certain that the 'new' service could support these ten young people in a way that prevented them from being admitted to care, otherwise the potential savings would disappear. One practical challenge in shifting resources away from residential care is the defined number of places in looked after services. These services are often working at full capacity, yet social workers still comment on the lack of places and the lack of choice in placements. How can expenditure savings in this low volume, high cost service be made today given this capacity constraint?

Other 'balance of care' questions quickly follow. How long should the period of double-running funding last? What tapering arrangements should be in place? What is the optimum level of 'preventative' services for which funding is required that will allow a sufficiently large impact on the future costs of looked after services? By how much can we reduce expenditure on high cost services without causing deterioration in current users' welfare? How quickly can these 'savings' be made and which bits of the budget should be sliced?

Thus studies in this initiative represent some of the first robust research-based knowledge about unit costs, the costs of support packages, and explorations about why costs vary. These variations mean that a considerable amount of choice is being exercised about how to provide services and how best to support children. As is the nature of research, many questions arise from the findings and much more information is needed in all these areas of cost-related research.

Summary

One of the requirements for studies funded under this initiative was to include a cost component. Developing new areas of unit costs was a crucial starting point with good progress made in looking at the costs of social care services, of social work processes, of multi-function services, and of collaboration. In many studies, these unit costs were used to construct information on care package costs. In some, care was taken to include costs that were 'hidden' to social services by virtue of coming from other agencies' budgets, or in one study the family purse. Other studies explored why the costs of ostensibly similar services – perhaps children's homes or family support services – vary so much.

There are three overarching findings.

First, the quality of information in case files on the use of services and supports is poor. Too many files had basic information on care history or school attendance missing. Easily available information on what supports children are using from a range of agencies will help service integration and improve the system's responsiveness to children's needs.

Second, these studies found that at the most, only a third of the variation in the costs of children's care could be explained statistically. What choices are local authorities making about how to spend money that have not been captured by these studies? Are some of these choices 'better' than others?

Finally, around 60 per cent of social services' resources are spent on placements for a relatively smaller number of looked after children. This may be a logical response to the very high needs of these children. But having more detail on how resources have been spent is helpful as directors of children's services consider how to spend their budget to be in line with the new Change for Children policy agenda.

Chapter 5

Interventions Unrelated to the Care System

Introduction

A key tenet of *Every Child Matters* is that interventions should be 'early'. What then is meant by early? An obvious answer is 'when the child is very young' and when later problems may be prevented. Social services departments, however, have often thought of prevention as primarily concerned with preventing the occurrence of problems so severe that they are likely to lead to a need for care. As we have seen in previous chapters this has in practice meant a concentration on children who are on the verge of being looked after, are currently looked after or have been looked after.

In this chapter we will focus on interventions that are *not* specifically targeted at those who might be, are, or have been looked after. Often such services are early in the sense that they are provided soon after problems first appear. However, we will also consider services for children with chronic problems who are not on the verge of being looked after.

The studies on which we will concentrate are all deliberately evaluative. This means that they aim to:

- describe the service and its clientele

- measure its outcomes

- relate outcomes to differences in or between services.

Our concerns will be fourfold. First, is there evidence that the service 'works' in the short term, and if so, in what way? Second, is it reasonable to think that it will prevent future 'poor outcomes'? Third, what does it cost? Fourth, does the study say anything about the service's cost-effectiveness?

Our understanding of what works is likely to depend on a combination of evidence. Ideally the service has an intelligible rationale, can be shown to engage its users, and has been positively evaluated in a number of studies using different designs.

In practice this latter criterion is rarely met. Evaluations of early intervention services are mainly American and their conclusions may not easily transfer to the

UK. Even if they do, the results seem somewhat conflicting and discouraging. A very tentative generalisation from this American research would be that:

- tightly controlled interventions with a clear rationale tend to have better outcomes than less strictly controlled 'standard' interventions
- it is easier to improve outcomes with younger children than with older ones.

So what do the studies in this initiative suggest?

Responsive services

For reasons that will become clearer as we continue, we distinguished between *responsive* and *specialist* services. *Responsive* services respond to the felt needs of their recipients. They are not tightly targeted on a 'high risk' population or on tightly specified needs. *Specialist* services attempt to engage recipients with defined characteristics in interventions whose desirability has been determined by professionals or politicians.

These broad distinctions tend to be associated with a number of others. In particular responsive services tend to occur earlier in a child's 'service career'; the closer the possibility that a child may need to be looked after the greater the chance that professionals have a predominant say in what the intervention should be about and whom it should serve. In this sense responsive services are not likely to fare well when assessed against tightly specified outcome measures defined by professionals. Instead they must to some extent respond to needs as a user defines them. If this was not so it is difficult to see why they should continue to use them.[1] This caveat should be borne in mind in understanding the results.

Obviously no intervention is entirely responsive or entirely specialist. Professionals have to provide some definition for even the most responsive service.[2] If they did not their users would not know what the service was for and would not know whether they wished to use it. At the other extreme a professional refusal to engage with the aims of users would almost certainly result in a service that was highly ineffective on any criterion. That said the distinction has relevance to the

---

1   For this reason an exclusive concentration on specialist services is likely to result in a wide range of unmet needs. This is partly because some needs will be given lower priority by professionals and partly because responsive services are often a gateway to specialist ones.

2   Home-Start provides a good example. We have treated it as a responsive service on the grounds that it is a response to the distress of the families and does not operate tight selection criteria or according to a highly developed theoretical rationale. On the other hand the health visitors who refer have a relatively clear idea of the kind of family suitable for Home-Start. Home-Start itself also has relatively clear ideas on the kind of changes it would like to see, a fact partly attested by its willingness to agree on outcome criteria with the researchers.

degree to which a service seeks to be easily accessible to the public, the extent to which it is rationed and the kinds of criteria against which it should be evaluated.

We begin with two interventions that we describe as 'responsive'.

Home-Start study

The Home-Start study set out to evaluate the effectiveness and costs of a family visiting service offered by Home-Start volunteers to families in 13 schemes in Northern Ireland and South East England. It involved 162 mothers, of whom 80 received the service and 82 lived in areas where Home-Start was not available. The research relied on Home-Start organisers and health visitors to identify the sample. The research was unusually successful in two respects. In terms of the families' characteristics and needs at the start of the study, the control sample was very similar to those receiving the visiting service and the researchers were able to retain a very high proportion (91%) within the study. Participants were interviewed on referral to the study (in the case of the 'intervention group' this corresponded to the start of the service) and one year later.

This study almost certainly dealt with one of the least deprived samples in the initiative. A relatively high proportion (69%) of them involved two-parent families with the age of the mothers ranging from 17 to 42. Around half the sample were living in their own housing and more than half were receiving income from employment. On average the families had three children and all had at least one child under five.

Despite their relative lack of deprivation the mothers were highly stressed. Around three-quarters experienced five or more serious stresses. These stresses were commonly related to parenting their children. Fifty-four per cent of the mothers said they had at least one child with special needs. Just over one in seven of the mothers said they had two or three such children. Yet despite these difficulties the mothers were, in general, receiving very little support from the mental health or other relevant services.

The experience or, more commonly repeated experience, of becoming a parent had hit the mothers hard. Postnatal depression, lack of sleep, isolation and the incessant demands of small children who often had special needs variously combined to leave many drained, lacking in self-esteem and feeling that they only existed to respond to the relentless demands of others. Many had given up work and faced a drop in income, some had physical problems of their own and others were in dispute with their partners or ex-partners over financial support and contact with children. As the report puts it: 'There was a strong sense of these mothers being overwhelmed at times by the intensity of the demands placed on them, particularly when trying to care for several children on their own. What seemed to make the situation particularly stressful was lack of respite.'

The mothers in the sample were interviewed at two points in time. At both points they completed various standard measures. At time one (when the mothers had been only briefly referred to Home-Start) the scores showed a considerable level of distress. Around two-thirds had a clinically significant level of parenting stress and around half seemed to be suffering medium to severe depression. By the end of the study there had been a considerable improvement on all scores in both groups. Similarly there had been considerable improvement in four of the five main problems they had identified (mental health, multiple demands, parenting issues/ child behaviour and lack of support). The exception was finance, a particular issue for lone parents. Just over half the parents initially reporting problems said there had been no change or even deterioration.

Qualitative information suggested that the reasons for this improvement were multiple. Parents were further away from the traumas, sleeplessness and upheavals surrounding birth. Anti-depressants had helped some, others had found that as their children grew up or moved to school the pressures were less, others had sorted out arrangements with partners resulting in more help for some and for others less hassle. Some felt they benefited from Home-Start support. Many simply grew more confident as parents, started to find routines and solutions that suited them, acquired more help from others and more child care and generally began to take control of their lives. The few to whom these improvements did not apply seemed to have more entrenched problems, for example, straitened financial circumstances or children with special needs who had not been assessed or for whom they were receiving no help.

Was this improvement a result of Home-Start's help? The vast majority of mothers reported that they had received one visit of approximately two hours per week. The visits provided emotional support, practical help and a chance for the mothers to get on with other things and, particularly towards the end of the contact, help with outings. Some mothers felt that the intensity of the service was insufficient to make a substantial difference to their everyday stresses, while others commented that what they had really wanted was a respite child care service not a home-visiting one. In general the mothers valued the help received but this praise contrasted with the quantitative results. Both the Home-Start and control groups improved sharply on all the main quantitative measures. Neither group improved more than the other.

The improvement in both groups suggests the need for a wide variety of responsive services. Home-Start was seen as helpful but even without it parents resolved some of their own difficulties. In doing so they may have received anti-depressants from their GPs, assessments of their children's impairments from hospital doctors, advice on debts or legal difficulties from the Citizen's Advice Bureau, advice on a wide variety of childhood difficulties from their health visitor, child care from local voluntary agencies and so on. The services the mothers needed are unlikely to be provided by just one agency. So their usefulness will depend on the ability of parents to access them[3] and of professionals in different agencies to collaborate together.

The lack of difference in outcome between the groups also highlights the risk of a positive opinion being confused with effectiveness. The parents receiving Home-Start support knew their visitors were volunteers and were no doubt grateful. They also liked them. Relatively few, however, attributed the improvement in their situation to Home-Start. So the good opinions they expressed may in part have flowed from their gratitude and liking. Asked whether they would spend the money devoted to these visits in other ways such as more childcare, they might have felt that it should. Many certainly wanted more respite from their children. Research into responsive services thus needs to pay close attention to what users think.

The study design, with data collected at the start and end of use of the service and with a comparison 'usual support' group, allowed cost and cost-effectiveness comparisons. The findings provide an interesting quandary for decision-makers. The costs of all services and supports were compared for the two groups. The group receiving Home-Start was more costly to support, in the main due to the extra cost associated with providing Home-Start services. Combined with the results of the quantitative outcome comparison, this places provision of Home-Start support in the top left-hand corner of our cost-effectiveness diagram (see Figure 2.1). This is where an equally effective but less costly 'usual support' dominates.

As we have seen, however, the mothers themselves might well dispute this decision. To what extent should commissioners use the more positive qualitative findings to move a decision about providing this service from the top left quadrant towards the top right (more effective but more costly)? The decision to commission Home-Start will depend on factors not studied here, for example, the availability of the voluntary organisation, perceived need for the service among their population and their local policies and priorities. It will also depend on whether they consider the positive opinions simply reflect liking and gratitude – and how important this is given other demands on their resources – or indicate subtle positive changes that the quantitative measures were not sufficiently refined to pick up. The difficulty in detecting results may also reflect the timing of the follow-up.[4]

---

3   This in turn may depend on information and on the provision of family-friendly, relevant services that open at convenient times and in convenient places.

4   It is possible that the Home-Start families recovered more quickly than the others who then 'caught up'. The follow-up may have been too late to detect this. Alternatively the effects may be cumulative over time so that a small initial difference is later magnified into a large one. In this case the follow-up may have been too early to detect the difference. Obviously it is very difficult to predict such subtleties of timing in advance.

So what is the case for extending this intervention? On the one hand it is logically related to the difficulties that it reduced. Those receiving Home-Start value it. It reduces isolation in a group that is going through a particularly difficult time. On the other, it does not reduce all the parents' problems; it may be less relevant to financial difficulties and the effect of children's impairments. Most of the mothers receiving it would probably have taken control of their own lives in any event, as they did in the comparison group. These findings point to the importance of being very clear about the outcomes we can expect from such a service and the value we place on them.

Therapeutic Family Support study

This study focused on 79 families who met the study criteria of being a new case in receipt of therapeutic services from a family support service and without a contact with the same service over the previous six months. All had to agree to take part in the research. An 'index child' (one focus of the research) was identified who had not reached the age of 13. The design of this study does not allow us to gauge 'absolute effectiveness' in that those who receive the service are not compared with a group that do not receive the service. Instead the study aims to explore how different components and characteristics of these 'multi-function' services had an impact on changes in users' health and welfare.

The 27 schemes[5] delivering the family support service came from both the voluntary and statutory sectors. They varied in therapeutic approach, in the degree to which they relied on self and professional referral and in whether they delivered their interventions in a centre or in people's homes. There were examples of schemes that tightly controlled their intake and operated according to quite specific therapeutic ideas, for example social learning theory. More generally they used a tool kit of approaches adapted to what they saw to be the needs of the client, and employed both group and individual work. The services were variously packaged and included, for example, parent pop-ins, family surgeries, crèches, cooking groups, planned activities, individual work with a child, parenting classes, planned activities, family therapy or family group conferences, groups of many kinds and attached volunteer schemes.

The workers included qualified social workers and family support workers, with the latter predominating and being more heavily represented in the statutory sector. Some of the work in which they were involved might seem to call for a high degree of training. On average families had contact with the staff about once a

5   The final sample came from 21 of these services.

week, and took part in a variety of activities such as counselling, group work, practical support, early years work, family work and parenting skills training.

The families recruited to the study were poor. Three-quarters subsisted on social security benefits. More than half involved a lone parent (54%) with the remainder being divided between birth parents (33%) and step-families (12.5%). Only 14 per cent owned their own homes. Their scores on a measure of family functioning were much worse than those of a community sample but similar to those of a sample of families attending a child and adolescent mental health service. They were in many respects 'chronically vulnerable'.

This vulnerability was associated with stressful events. Nearly half those in the study said they had been unemployed or seeking work or had a partner in this position during the previous six months.[6] Only slightly fewer had financial difficulties or trouble with the law. Over half had moved house in the previous six months, a third through choice, but a third involuntarily. Eighty per cent of the families had experienced four or more of such negative life events in the previous six months. Unsurprisingly the main carers were stressed with around half appearing significantly so on a standard measure of mental health.[7]

These stresses were not the immediate reason for referral. In around a fifth of cases there were concerns about child protection. Slightly less often referrals were related to parental mental health. However the most common reason for referral was the child's behaviour problems (45%). On a standard measure 81 per cent of the children scored in the abnormal range for conduct problems and a further 6 per cent were in the borderline range.

The study measured a variety of outcomes including the child's behaviour and mental health, the carer's level of stress and self-esteem, the way the family worked and the size and levels of support provided by their social network. On most outcomes there was, on average, no significant change, although over time the children appeared to have fewer problems with their peers and to have become, according to their carers, more 'pro-social'. This 'average' disguised the fact that some families improved, some stayed the same and some deteriorated. This variation was most obvious in relation to the measures of stress and self-esteem. These were strongly related to the experience of difficult events in the recent past. Families that received strong social support also improved on family functioning and had children who came to show more 'pro-social' behaviour. By contrast older children showed less improvement (or more deterioration) in behaviour.

---

6   Families were asked about problems in the last six months. Some may have included earlier events in their answers.

7   The measure used relies on a response 'worse than usual' that arguably leads those with chronic stress to rate themselves as better than their mental health might appear to warrant.

Did the characteristics of the services affect the outcomes? Rather little it seemed. The researchers took account of the users' characteristics and needs on entry to the service. Once this had been done there was in general no evidence that the training of the workers, the extent or nature of the intervention or its source had any differential impact on outcome.[8] This is, perhaps, not what might be expected if the intervention was a powerful one.[9] Disappointingly, given the person-to-person nature of children's social care services, there was no evidence that the quality of therapeutic alliance[10] between worker and family was related to any outcome variable, with the possible exception of a measure of family functioning.

One innovative and very interesting feature of the study lay in its attempts to measure the degree to which various specific goals had been attained. These goals were highly varied including, for example, 'to get off drugs' or 'to take part in some voluntary activity'. Many workers felt that a goal-oriented approach was not appropriate to their work. Others felt that goals were appropriate but found it hard to define them. Where goals had been agreed clients generally felt that there had been at least some progress towards most of them. For example, one mother said that her child's behaviour had not improved but that she realised that she was no longer alone. Another was delighted that her child's enuresis had improved. Neither of these outcomes would necessarily show up in the standardised, quantitative measures used.

The findings on goal attainment suggest that a service may be successful in achieving a wide variety of specific outcomes without, on average, changing overall well-being. In general the clients spoke well of the interventions, trusted the workers and felt that they were consulted and could raise issues of concern if they needed to. These high ratings do not necessarily imply effectiveness, however, they do suggest that being clearer about what it is that the service and family together might achieve may be a useful way of assessing how 'effective' a service might be.

The absence of a comparison group receiving different or no services means we cannot tell whether therapeutic family services meant more – or less – costly support packages were put in place. If the case for cost-effectiveness remains

---

8   There were some rather curious findings on the associations between outreach work, a service provided by a voluntary agency and carer stress. Outreach was associated with some negative outcomes. It is possible that this reflects the fact that those who attended centres to receive counselling would have been more motivated than those whose families received counselling from a worker who visited them. Those served by a voluntary agency seemed to do worse in terms of behaviour problems. The significance level of this finding is quite low and it has no obvious explanation.

9   It is, of course, compatible with a powerful intervention. However, one would not, for example, expect powerful medical interventions to be equally efficacious irrespective of dosage or whether the practitioner had been trained in them.

10 This measured the users' beliefs about their worker's skill, their bond with the worker and the extent to which the family and worker were in agreement about the benefits of the intervention.

unproven, can the findings from the cost-related analyses provide indications of the way forward for commissioners or managers?

Alongside careful estimation of the cost of therapeutic family supports (see Chapter 4), information on the main health, special education and social services was collected and care package costs estimated. Over the six-month period there was no increase or decrease in the quantity or range of other services used overall. The researchers also explored whether different ways of delivering the service had any impact. They looked at the sector in which the service was managed and whether the child saw a qualified social worker. There was some evidence to suggest that the voluntary sector services, which were more likely to have an open access policy, acted as a referring agency to other statutory services. On the whole, however, family support provided an additional, not a replacement service. The services would probably increase the total support costs for user families' although by a fairly small amount.

So what, on the basis of this study, can be said for these therapeutic interventions? On the positive side they are targeted at a very needy population, and generally well regarded by the users willing to become involved in research. They may well achieve specific goals for some families. On the negative side many of the interventions seem to have very little theoretical rationale. Moreover they are delivered by staff who do not necessarily have the training commonly expected of those delivering this kind of support, and to families whose 'chronic' difficulties may well make any substantive change very difficult to achieve.

Some issues for responsive services

A 'preventive' agenda depends on the identification and effective treatment of problems likely to lead to later difficulties.

Families and children do not necessarily share this agenda. These have a wide variety of felt needs. Some needs may be unlikely to lead to later difficulties while others may not be amenable to intervention. The sheer variety of needs that a service may be aiming to meet may mean that it does not appear as particularly effective in dealing any specific one.

In keeping with this the services we described as 'responsive' did not appear particularly effective in the terms set out by the researchers. They were, however, relatively low cost services and they were popular with their users.

As with Home-Start, these services provide relatively low cost interventions (here between 3 and 10% of the total support costs), but are they a good investment? We do not know. We have as yet we have no way of assessing their longer-term impact. Strictly speaking we cannot say that these interventions were 'ineffective', even taking into account the 'no change' finding on the quantitative measures. There was no comparison group to confirm whether this service worked as well as another. We do not know if these families would, on average, have deteriorated without this service. In some cases maintenance of the current position may itself be an achievement.

That said, the lack of positive changes contrasts with the findings of the study of adolescent teams (see Chapter 6). It is also disappointing that outcomes were not related to relationships with users or to the characteristics of the services. This is contrary to what one might expect if the services were having a powerful influence. We need to think carefully about what we expect these services to achieve and how we measure it.

Specialist services

Some of the projects in the Therapeutic Family Support study operated according to tightly defined criteria and with specific treatment rationales. Most did not. In the next section we will look at two studies of 'specialist' services. Both these services had tightly defined methods of operation. Both set out to recruit a tightly defined target population for whom they believed the service would be effective. Both had aims that could broadly be described as 'preventive'.

Earlier overviews have rarely covered studies of this kind of service or those using this kind of research design. One, however, was covered and seemed particularly important. This SPOKES project was targeted on young children at the beginning of their primary school career (years one and two). The children were selected on the basis of standard measures suggesting that they had serious difficulties and randomly divided into two groups, one receiving the intervention and the other an offer of less intensive support. The parents in the 'intensive arm' were invited to take part in a three-term course designed to help them handle their child's behaviour and relationship with them and help the child with reading. Great efforts were made to engage the parents in the courses and parents were highly appreciative of them. The results of the study were very encouraging with significant reductions in anti-social and other difficult behaviours for those using the intervention.[11]

---

11   There is as yet no information that compares the costs of these supports. A recent report reviews both effectiveness and economic evidence for parenting programmes: Dretzke *et al.* 2005.

This project had a number of characteristics that might have been expected to contribute to its success:

- It was targeted at relatively young children at the beginning of their school career, a group who may find it easier to change than older children more set in their ways and with their school reputations already established.

- It was delivered in a way that was non-stigmatising and that engaged parents.

- It had a clear rationale, being based in part on the positively evaluated approach of Dr Webster-Stratton, and was targeted at relationships between the child and two key determinants of their well-being: their family and their school.

- It drew on techniques of parent and literacy training for which there was already evidence and which had some theoretical grounding.

- Those delivering the intervention had the training and qualifications required for these particular interventions.

In assessing the study descriptions that follow it is useful to ask how far these interventions had such favourable conditions. We discuss the relevant studies in the order of the average age of the children they studied. The first began before the children had even been born.

Health Visiting study

This study focused on a sample of women referred by midwives attached to 40 GP practices in the study area. All the women had at least one 'marker' of risk.[12] In addition they had to be willing to be involved in research that included random allocation.

The 131 parents who met these criteria were randomly allocated to a special visiting service (n=68) or to treatment as usual (n=63). These groups represented about a third of a much larger group who had been identified by midwives as at risk, about two-thirds of whom had agreed to take part in the project. However, to ensure the service would be targeted on those they thought would benefit most, the researchers excluded about half of those agreeing to take part as they did not fully meet the criteria. A further 11 per cent then declined to take part in the study. This drop-out rate partly reflected a reluctance to take part in the intervention and partly

---

12   Age less than 17; serious housing problems or no accommodation; serious financial difficulties; isolated with no support network; history of psychiatric illness; learning problems; serious drug or alcohol problems in the past; serious parenting difficulties or child on the child protection register; domestic violence; been referred to a social worker.

a reluctance to take part in the study. A small number of interviews with those who reached a relatively late stage in the process before declining suggested a variety of reasons. Some, for example, did not understand what was offered, some were too distressed to consider it, others did not trust services, others felt the service inappropriate, some feared losing their current service and so on. Whatever the reason it appears that such a service is unlikely to engage everyone.

The groups who did take part were followed up at six months and 12 months after the birth of their child. In addition the researchers explored the experience of the mothers through interviews and that of those delivering the intervention through focus groups.

The health visitors involved in the special service had eight days of training designed to help them form strong partnerships with parents and in techniques such as infant massage that they could teach the parents. The aim was to enable the parents to be more sensitive to their babies, to improve their relationships with them and to solve particular parenting problems. The assumptions were that both baby and parent were social beings who made sense of their world through social constructs that would have to be modified if their relationship was not going well.[13] The approach was embodied in a manual, and reinforced by twice-a-month group supervision for health visitors, and individual sessions with a clinical supervisor as required. A clinical advisory group was available to provide advice on particular issues. The intervention began up to six months before the baby was born and lasted for up to 18 months.

The special visiting group were very similar in their characteristics to the others. By contrast they had a markedly different experience of the support provided. Very few dropped out from the intervention and on average they received 41.2 as against 9.2 visits for those in the usual treatment group. Despite some initial opposition the parents' attitudes were very favourable to the special visiting service to which many of them gave moving tributes. The health visitors were similarly positive, feeling that they had been given both the time and the skills to deliver a very superior service, albeit one which sometimes had personal costs to themselves. Both the health visitors and the users gave particular emphasis to the trusting relationships that had developed.

As with the two studies described above, the statistical results were less conclusive. On average there were few differences in outcome at follow-up at two, six and 12 months. Differences on most measures favoured the intervention group but only two of the main measures were statistically significant: the mothers were more

---

13   Health visitors, for example, would encourage mothers to think how their baby might respond to something the mothers were doing. This approach was designed to get the mother to think of the baby as a 'social being'.

sensitive to their babies and the infants were more co-operative with them.[14] In the longer term, much depends on whether this difference is transient, disappearing when the higher level of support stops, or whether it marks the beginning of a benign cycle whereby mother and child take increasing delight in each other.

In the short term the special visiting service changed the costs of other services. The mothers using the specialist service cost less to the accident and emergency services, but more to the psychology service. However, this specialist service is unlikely to reduce the load on the care system. If anything the reverse is likely to be the case. The number of children removed to the care system was greater (albeit not significantly greater) in the group receiving the special service.[15] The researchers regarded this as a positive feature of the service for families at risk, ensuring a speedier 'specialist' response to children in difficulty. We shall see in the next chapter how some studies point to the cumulative problems caused by delayed decision-making about entering the care system.

The combination of the higher costs to the care system and the higher costs of the more intensive health visitor service meant that overall, the costs of supporting mothers using the specialist service were considerably higher than for the 'usual service' group; by just over £3000 over the study period. Only about a quarter of this additional cost was borne by the care system, with the remainder absorbed by the additional health visitor costs. One cost-effectiveness analysis used a measure of 'the time infants were exposed to the risk of neglect'. The results showed that the special health visiting service was almost always more costly, but always more effective in reducing the time at risk. Further analysis[16] showed that if decision-makers are willing to spend £2500 to reduce the risk of an infant's exposure to neglect by one month, then there is a 90 per cent probability that the special health visiting service is more cost-effective than a routine service. The idea behind this type of analysis is to give the decision-makers more information. The concept of 'uncertainty' was discussed in Chapters 1 and 2. This analysis identifies how 'certain' the researcher is about the findings. This helps decision-makers in their trade-off between likely outcomes and the prices they might have to pay.

In the short term, the new specialist service was more effective, however, such a service is predicated on a longer-term impact, so strictly speaking it is necessary to withhold judgement. It is not possible to say how far its results will outlast the immediate phase of intervention. It is, however, a closely defined intervention. If

---

14   Strictly speaking these were part of a single 'main measure'. There were two other main measures.

15   Four children were removed in the intervention group and none in the treatment as usual group. The latter, however, included a child who died. In this case there were child protection concerns and the coroner recorded an open verdict.

16   The statistical estimation of a cost effectiveness acceptability curve.

the intervention manual is followed closely and if it is implemented using the same inclusion criteria then the short-term findings should be reproduced. It is also apparent that the service is very popular, it makes sense, and individuals who have appropriate training deliver it. As with many of the studies in this initiative, further studies are needed to substantiate the findings.

Sexual Abuse study

This study focused on 75 children aged 6 to 14 years who were referred to one of two London centres. All had, on the balance of probabilities, been sexually abused, all were female, and all had psychological symptoms of such severity that they warranted treatment. With their carers' agreement the children were randomly allocated to one of two groups, one to receive up to 18 sessions of a group treatment ('psycho-educational group therapy') and the other up to 30 sessions of individual 'focused' psychotherapy with a psychoanalytic base. Both groups were offered family support from a social worker. Fifty-eight children were followed up after one year, 54 after two years, and 66 were interviewed at least once.

The results showed that on a measure of overall mental health functioning both groups improved substantially and to a roughly equal extent. However, there was evidence that on at least one measure related to post-traumatic stress disorder the improvement was significantly greater in the group receiving individual treatment. Overall costs were significantly greater in the group receiving individual therapy – a difference over the treatment period of £1246.

The cost-effectiveness analysis funded through this initiative and the previously published findings from the outcome analysis reflect rather different 'takes' on these results. The outcomes analysis emphasises the superior performance of the individual approach in relation to post-traumatic stress disorder, although the researchers note that the small sample size limits the strength of this conclusion (Trowel et al. 2002).

The costs and cost-effectiveness analysis concentrated on the overall outcome results, rather that those for post-traumatic stress disorder. It therefore suggested that as the superiority of one treatment over the other is unproved there is little to choose between the two treatments in terms of outcome. In this situation, more complex analyses were not needed to show that group therapy can be placed towards the bottom right-hand quadrant of the cost-effectiveness diagram in Figure 2.1. With similar outcomes produced for less expenditure, group therapy is the more cost-effective option.

As with the paper on outcomes there are uncertainties. As the authors say, not only is the sample small, but also only the costs associated with therapy (including assessment for therapy, meetings, supervision, and the linked family support) are considered. If the costs borne by all other agencies were included, such as the use of social care services or additional education support, the results may not have been the same.

What can be made of these findings? From a cautious scientific point of view it is hard to evaluate the significance of the differences that were found. The difference relating to post-traumatic stress disorder is statistically significant. It may or may not be sufficiently great to be important for the individuals involved. More importantly the two interventions differed in the settings, the experience and theoretical orientations of the professionals involved, in the speed with which the interventions were delivered, and much else besides. So it is unclear whether it is, for example, the nature of the therapists or the nature of the treatment that produced any differences. Strictly speaking the major differences related to changes over time, so one could argue that the children were first contacted at a particularly difficult point in their lives and that things were only likely to get better after that.

From a practical point of view it is doubtful if practitioners can afford to take such a sceptical attitude. The researchers themselves argue that both the interventions probably were effective. Previous research suggests that these children would have been unlikely to improve on their own without active intervention. The children themselves were clearly in serious difficulty. Practitioners may well consider it unacceptable to leave such a child without treatment simply because there is a possibility that an intervention may not work for them.

Some issues for specialist services

Some specialist services dealt with a defined clientele with a view to obtaining defined outcomes according to a specified rationale. The results for these services were undoubtedly promising. It remained uncertain whether the good results:

- would last or indeed improve over time
- would be replicated if the service was implemented more widely
- would save money for other services – leastways in the short term.

Fortunately the results of both the Health Visiting and the SPOKES study were, at the least, consistent with those of other research. This should reassure those considering the development of services of this kind, while not diminishing the need for further research into them.

The sensible way forward would therefore be to offer an intervention and to prefer group treatment where practicable as the cheaper option. At the same time it has to be realised that the 'uncertainty' around these findings means that group treatment may be worse than an individual approach, or better for some children and worse for others. It is possible that neither treatment makes a difference. So it is important not only that practitioners act on the evidence currently available but also that they actively support research designed to reduce these uncertainties.

Conclusion

What case can be made for the interventions described in this chapter? As we have seen they have included:

- a low intensity responsive service for groups with mainly transient difficulties (Home-Start study)

- a medium intensity responsive service intended to relieve specific difficulties defined by the user (Therapeutic Family Support study)

- two medium intensity specialist and proactive services delivered by trained staff according to a defined rationale and to groups thought likely to change (SPOKES and Health Visiting study)

- a medium intensity specialist service delivered to users with chronic problems by trained staff operating according to a defined rationale and evaluated according to their ability to resolve these chronic problems (Sexual Abuse study).

So do the services work? And if so, at what cost? The answers depend on what outcomes are valued and what emphasis is put on which evidence.

The case for the two responsive services – Home-Start volunteers and therapeutic family services – is essentially threefold: users like them; those who receive them are in considerable distress; the services are relatively low cost when compared with others. However, the studies have not shown conclusively that these services are effective, and for the Home-Start study the evidence suggests it is no more effective than the comparison service.

In part this may be because the concept of effectiveness is dependent on that of intention. In both studies the main measures the researchers selected to assess changes in user well-being showed that on average users did improve over time (albeit in the case of the therapeutic family support services only slightly and in relation to particular difficulties), but that this could not be ascribed to the service or its characteristics. Users may well see things very differently.

If the question is 'do these responsive services prevent the poor outcomes that may lead to admission into the care system' then the answer is more complex. Few users of these services appear to have characteristics that render them liable to entry to the care system, and the services themselves do not appear to be targeted on these groups. However, these 'low-level' early interventions may have a long-term impact on preventing the precursors of such characteristics. This as yet cannot be gauged.

We called the other two services 'specialist' – those in the Health Visiting and Sexual Abuse studies. These services are also delivered to families or young people in considerable difficulty, but both are targeted at very specific groups. The services themselves have a defined rationale. Those who deliver them have appropriate training. The results are in keeping with other evaluations of parent training programmes and family visiting.

Against this background and despite the numerous uncertainties it is likely that these specialist services 'work': outcomes for children improved. Admittedly they probably did not prevent 'admission to care'. Few of those involved were at risk of this and insofar as any were, the provision of these services may have hastened (perhaps appropriately) this event. The longer-term effects are uncertain but certainly worth evaluating. It does seem likely, however, that the immediate changes in well-being at which the services aimed will lead on to other positive outcomes.[17] The children were probably at risk of a wide range of different 'poor outcomes' and it may well be the case that some of these outcomes were prevented.

Summary

This chapter looks at the studies that evaluated services that were not primarily targeted at children who were 'at risk' of being looked after, were being looked after or had been looked after.

The chapter considers two 'responsive' services, Home-Start and therapeutic family support services, and two specialist services – intensive health visiting and psychotherapy for sexually abused girls. The distinction between responsive and specialist services is not always clear-cut but the former tend to respond to the felt needs of their recipients, often dealing with a wide range of needs. Specialist services are more tightly

---

17   The case for believing this is well made in the report on the Health Visiting study. American studies of early interventions have discovered such 'sleeper' effects. These are likely where a small strategic change could be expected to have cumulative benefits over time. For example, the fact that children do not fall behind with reading may mean that they do not find their lessons more and more confusing as time goes on with consequences for their confidence and for their role in the school. Similarly a small change in children's relationships with their mothers could lead to a benign spiral with more and more positive benefits.

targeted and attempt to engage recipients in interventions deemed useful by professionals.

The case for the two responsive services is threefold: users like them, those who receive them are in considerable distress and they are relatively low cost. The researchers were not able to show that either service was able to improve standard outcomes. On balance, the findings for the two specialist services were more encouraging. Mothers preferred the intensive service to ordinary health visiting, and outcomes for children probably improved albeit at a greater cost. Both group and individual psychotherapy are effective with the former probably more cost-effective. For both studies, associated evidence suggests that the small immediate changes will lead onto other positive outcomes.

In general it appeared very unlikely that any of these services would reduce the use of the care system in the immediate future. If anything they would be likely to increase demand for care as children's problems are brought to light. Whether these services will have a long-term impact on reducing use of the care system remains unknown. For the moment, however, the arguments for them seem to be that they are popular and have good effects, not that they save money in the long run.

Chapter 6

Interventions Related to the Care System

Introduction

This chapter deals with studies of children who had either been in the care system, were currently in the system or were on the verge of it. In our terms these very vulnerable children were the targets of 'later interventions'.

As we have seen these later interventions absorb a high proportion of the resources of social services departments. This situation seems hard to change. We have argued that it may have been, in a sense, part of the destiny of social services. This does not mean that the successors of these departments may not be able to fulfil this destiny more effectively or more cost-effectively. These are the issues to which we now turn.

We look first at studies that bear particularly on assessment, planning and the provision of services. We then look at studies of community-based services that aim to prevent admission to care or support those leaving care. Finally we look at studies of adoption, foster carers and children's homes. In this way we cover a great portion of the work with children that has been carried by social services departments.

Assessment and care planning

Some children and young people receive services for only a short period. Others receive more services, and often more costly ones, over a long period. The 'decisions' that result in these different service careers are clearly crucial, both for the services and for the children themselves. Three studies, the Assessment Framework study, the Care Careers study and the Adoption study were particularly relevant to these key decision points.

Assessment Framework study

The researchers examined the introduction of the new 'Assessment Framework' in 24 local authorities. Their findings were informed by their work in developing the framework and offering some advice and training to the authorities in the study. More formally they combined an audit of assessment records, postal questionnaires to social workers, managers and practitioners, and case studies to develop a descriptive-analytic approach to evaluating the framework's implementation. They also calculated the cost of core assessments.

Overall their study illustrated both the advantages and the difficulties of assessments. On the positive side, initial assessments were often well completed. Some social workers and managers[1] felt that the new system produced better, more systematic assessment that looked at need as well as risk, made it easier for managers to monitor work and find information, and promoted communication with users. Case studies suggested that some users responded positively to the system.[2] Some professionals outside social services felt that the use of the system achieved one of its aims, to clarify roles, and that it made collaboration easier.

Many of the difficulties were about implementing the system. The majority of managers and social workers saw the system as taking up time. Small numbers also felt that clients experienced it as intrusive, that it required information that might not be necessary and that it was, in certain respects, inappropriate for disabled users. Lack of resources was seen by outside professionals as one of the factors that limited collaboration. Some professionals commented that the system required a mechanical 'questionnaire' approach to assessment; a view that the researchers felt was a misunderstanding. The audit of records showed a number of difficulties including incomplete assessments and a failure to link plans with evidence.

The researchers point to conditions that may promote these generally encouraging findings for staff and families. They were more likely to occur where the senior management were committed and saw the place of the new assessment system in their overall strategy. A project manager and an inter-agency group helped the introduction process. So too did good working relationships with other agencies at both practice and strategic levels, including joint protocols for inter-agency assessment and referral. To move from assessment to action a full range of services was needed from which courses of action could be selected.

---

1   As is almost inevitable in such 'engaged' projects response rates were sometimes low and the degree of bias hard to determine. Much of the analysis is based on hard won experience as well as formal research.

2   The sample was small and those agreeing to take part in interviews may have had unusually favourable experiences. Equally the sample had to be volunteered by social workers who may have been reluctant to refer problematic cases. In practice the evidence on assessment in this study seems to have been somewhat equivocal. Three-quarters of managers replying and 42 per cent of the professionals believed that the introduction of the assessment framework had improved family involvement. By contrast a third of the social workers believed that it had hindered family involvement, only 10 per cent of family assessment records included a signature of a family member and only a fifth of the records made any reference to family concerns.

Within social services there was a need for appropriate written guidance for families and social workers, information technology with sufficient capacity and appropriate training. To make best use of the Assessment Framework, social workers required basic knowledge of child development and how to assess in accordance with it. During the Framework's introduction, supervision and training should be focused on the system but an ongoing training programme was also needed to take into account the turnover of staff, the use of agency staff and the deficiencies of some basic training. Finally the researchers report that the operation of the system has to be continuously monitored.

Adoption study

The Adoption study focused on 130 children for whom a best interest decision (should be placed for adoption recommendation) had been made in the 1990s. On average they had been in adoptive placements for about seven years. The children were aged 3–11 at the time of the decision. Overall 96 had been placed with adopters, 80 were still with them, 34 were fostered and 16 had not achieved any stable placement. The researchers used case files and interviews with carers and the adoptive family to examine the reasons for these differences in careers and outcomes.

The children's birth parents had multiple overlapping problems with domestic violence, mental health problems and drug or alcohol abuse as common features. Sixty-three per cent of the birth mothers had been in care and 32 per cent already had a child looked after or adopted. A Schedule 1 offender was living in or frequently visiting 32 per cent of the birth homes and of these offenders 80 per cent had attached themselves to a mother with learning difficulties. Concerns about the parent's capacity to care for a new baby began before or shortly after birth for 63 per cent of the children. Most of the children (90%) experienced abuse and neglect whilst living at home with 68 per cent experiencing multiple forms of abuse.

The researchers were critical of the support given to the birth families. Intensive support at home was sometimes discontinued when the families' problems had not diminished. The result was that the child was still unable to remain at home but adoption was delayed. In the researchers' view there was much unjustified delay (sometimes related to the courts and sometimes to social work practice), assessments lacked focus, interventions continued without review and without success, and plans to return the children home were not implemented.

Over time the behavioural problems of the children became more pronounced. Delays in entering the care system, delays in coming to a decision over adoption, learning difficulties and overt sexualised behaviour in young children all reduced the chances that a child would be adopted. Children's level of violent behaviour was, independent of other factors, a powerful predictor of outcome. The chances of being adopted reduced by nearly a half for every year of delay. The researchers calculated the costs to the social services department of delaying the best interest decision. Where the decision was made and implemented quickly, children had spent an average of 26 weeks in foster care. The average cost for these children (n=48) between becoming looked after and the best interest decision was £8900. In contrast, 11 children in the study had waited more than five years before the best interest decision was made. The average cost for these children, including two who spent time in residential care, was £94,550. Failed attempts at rehabilitation increased the chance that a child would have an unstable care career and also resulted in increased social services' costs (see Box 6.1).

Box 6.1 An example of the importance of assessment

In the Adoption study there were 16 children who by the follow-up had experienced multiple disruptions and whose behaviour was so challenging that many were being cared for in specialist residential care. Their lives were sad stories with the majority not expected to live within the community as adults. Fourteen of these children had been referred to a social services department at the time of their birth. With the benefit of hindsight, it was possible to identify from case files decision points that might have changed their pathways.

Inadequate assessments played a major role in failing to identify specific conditions. At an early stage, the behaviours exhibited by these children were either unusual or extreme and merited a thorough investigation. In practice, however, they had received fewer diagnoses than the other children. Little attention had apparently been paid to their educational needs. Half had been excluded from school for long periods and the other half had been truants. Over a quarter of the children were of above average intelligence, yet none of those who had left school had any qualifications.

Once in the care system their difficulties did not escape notice. There were reports on file of futile attempts by teachers, carers and social workers to draw attention to their plight and secure specialist help. This however, was rarely forthcoming. In particular CAMHS refused to work with children who were not in a stable placement.

The researchers identified the costs of these children's care careers to social services.

- By April 2001–2 social services costs for each of the 16 'unstable' children were on average around £521,000.

- These placement costs can be compared with those for the 34 children who had achieved some permanency through non-adoptive placements (£186,000).

Overall, these cases highlighted the crucial importance of both assessment and the ability to respond.

The implications of this study are not straightforward. The nature of the sample meant that those whose return home succeeded were very unlikely to be included. The study therefore highlights the risks rather than the successes of rehabilitation. Clearly it would be quite unacceptable for all children at risk to be placed for adoption: on the other hand the downside of failed attempts is clearly very considerable. The study therefore points to:

- the fallible nature of all assessments and the need for fall-back plans such as 'parallel planning', and for continued monitoring

- the dependence of all assessments on adequate resources to implement support plans – in this case sources of intensive and appropriate family support that can last for as long as needed

- the need for all parties in assessment to 'sing from the same hymn sheet' – in this study the courts and guardians ad litem were also significant sources of adoption delay

- the crucial nature of the assessments and decisions both for 'downstream costs' and – more importantly – for the lives of the children concerned

- the need for these decisions to be made quickly and based on a thorough and accurate assessment.

Care Careers study

The Care Careers study focused on 478 children aged ten and over who had been looked after in six authorities in the week of the Children in Need survey 2000. The study described the authorities and provided qualitative data on the experiences of some of the children involved. Its primary purpose, however, was to explore the costs of different possible 'pathways' through the care system and the factors that influenced them. For this reason most of the findings have been presented in earlier chapters. Combined, however, with the other two studies in this section it underpins some general points about assessment, illustrating in particular that the 'funnelling' process that takes place outside the care system also occurs within it. Those who were returning home tended to do so relatively soon after arrival, while many of the others remained for a long time in the system.

Overall, the studies suggest that:

- even core assessments are relatively cheap when compared with the resource implications of the decisions they influence (6, 13, 14)

- poor assessment of children receiving very expensive resources may mean that they fail to receive relatively inexpensive but badly needed help (6, 14)

- assessment should not be seen as a 'one-off' event but should reflect cumulative experience and review (13)

- the outcomes of assessments depend on the quality of practice (6), the availability of appropriate resources (6, 13) and other contextual factors such as the views of courts (6,13) or the planning arrangements (14)

- successful introduction of a new system of assessment will be helped by a variety of organisational factors, as well as continuous training and monitoring (6).

Community services

The initiative examined two community services that were explicitly related to the care system. The first was intended to prevent adolescents from becoming looked after. The second was concerned with care leavers.

Adolescent Prevention study

The Adolescent Prevention study evaluated the work of specialist support teams for adolescents, set up to divert young people from the care system. The researchers compared 144 young people served by the specialist teams with 65 other adolescents in the same or other authorities who received the mainstream social work service. All the young people were aged 11–16. They only entered the study if they or their parents were asking for a period of 'care' or the social workers thought this might be necessary. The researchers followed them up for six months from the point of referral, interviewing young people and parents at both points and collecting information from the relevant workers.

The young people and their parents proved to have very severe difficulties, with over three-quarters of the young people and three-quarters of their parents scoring 'poorly' on different measures of mental health. The families were marked by domestic violence, family disputes and concerns about the neglect or physical abuse of the young person. Parents were worn down by relentless arguments and a cycle of mutual rejection, violence and abuse. Ninety-eight per cent of the young people had problems of behaviour including running away from home (76%), truancy (66%), petty theft from families (51%) and violence within (48%) and outside (41%) the family. Sizeable minorities had problems relating to drug or alcohol abuse, self-harm and sexual behaviour. In the great majority of cases the problems had lasted for more than a year and in a sizeable minority of cases they had lasted for more than three.

The specialist teams had a similar, if possibly more difficult, clientele to that of the mainstream teams but offered a briefer but much more intensive service. The specialist teams closed their cases on average after five as against nine months with a much higher number of face-to-face contacts in the first six months (33 hours as against 11 hours). Their workers visited up to three times a week in the early stages and provided an eclectic mix of interventions, for example, offering strategies to the young people and parents to control their behaviour and mediating between parents and the young person.

One striking set of findings related to improvements in the sample as a whole. Over the period of follow-up:

- the proportion of parents suffering significant psychological distress fell from 72 per cent to 38 per cent, and between one-third and two-thirds reported improvements on most of the specific difficulties mentioned at referral

- young people became much more likely to consider their situation improved and the proportion with high levels of emotional and behavioural problems dropped from 76 per cent to 55 per cent

- the greatest improvement was in relation to violence to parents but there was little change in offending, school exclusion or self-harm.

Comparing the outcomes for the two kinds of team the researchers found that:

- there were no differences between the teams in the psycho-social outcomes for the young people

- the specialist teams may have had greater success in engaging unmotivated young people and their services were more highly appreciated

- A significantly lower proportion of children served by the specialist teams were looked after on a 'long-term' basis (6% compared with 29%).

There is a contrast between the entrenched and long-standing nature of many problems shown by the young people in this study and the marked improvement six months later. Arguably they are a group that is chronically vulnerable to crises. The effects of these on morale and family relationships dissipate over a relatively brief time. However, the fact that the problems seemed chronic suggests that they were likely to reoccur.

The study design does not allow us to tell whether or not these young people would have improved if they had not received a service at all – the difficulties of the young people and families diminished irrespective of which intervention they received. That said, the families undoubtedly welcomed the services and complained bitterly of the years in which they had soldiered on without significant help from anyone.

If both specialist and mainstream social work teams generated similar psycho-social outcomes for the young people and their families, can the economic evaluation throw any light on decisions that have to be taken about supporting this group of young people?

The cost perspective was broad (see Chapter 4). Interestingly, it was more difficult to follow up young people using the mainstream service (more of whom entered the care system) than those using the specialist teams. This meant there were more young people for whom costs could not be calculated in that group so statistical adjustments were made. A comparison of mean costs and effectiveness found the two services to be similar; on average the care packages cost the same and the scores on the quality of life measure were also similar.

The researchers also showed how the relationship between costs and outcomes varied between young people. While information about mean costs is of greatest use to planners[3] it is also important to recognise that this 'average' may disguise important variations in costs for different young people. The researchers used a scatter plot to illustrate this variation. It showed that specialist support teams might, perhaps, be a more cost-effective form of support for some young people; other young people may be equally well served by the more usual social work approach. More work is clearly needed to find out 'for whom, and under what circumstances this service is a cost-effective option'.

What on balance can be said for the specialist prevention team? On the positive side the findings suggests that setting up such a service is necessary to help many of the families get a service at all. It was probably better at engaging 'hard to reach' families and adolescents. Engaging people is a necessary condition for an effective service. While it is not manifestly more effective than the mainstream alternative, it is more popular with its users, and shows less reliance on long-term care.[4] As on average the users of the specialist teams received care packages at no higher cost than the mainstream service users, there seems much to be said for them.

Care Leavers study

This study started at the time the Children (Leaving Care) Act in 2001 was being implemented and was designed to explore how care leavers were supported. It recruited a sample of 106 care leavers in seven local authorities. The researchers followed them up nine to ten months later. They used statistical techniques and case studies to understand the factors that led to various outcomes and identify what helped.

In general the study identified a complex process whereby the young people's difficulties in mental health and education and were associated both with each other and with events in their lives. These could lead to further difficulties. For

---

3   It allows them to 'multiply up' to estimate the support costs for a whole population of similar young people.

4   This difference does not necessarily mean that the specialist terms prevented the young people from entering the care system. The transfer of resources from residential care to community care may simply have meant that there were fewer placements for young people. Of course it could still be argued that the specialist teams were superior because they provided support in a way that was less likely to require the removal of the young person from their family.

example young people with challenging behaviour and shorter, more unsettled care careers were more likely to leave care at 16 or 17, rather than later. This in turn seemed to make them more likely to be unemployed at follow-up. Unemployment was also more likely among those who had unstable housing, poor life and social skills, and troubled lives.

Against this background continuing contact with personal advisers was high – 97 per cent of the young people were still in touch at follow-up and for 60 per cent contact was monthly or more. This seemed in some respects a 'fire-fighting' service. Contact was more common among those who experienced difficulties. Un-surprisingly, therefore, more contact was not associated with good outcomes. This did not, however, mean that the contact was ineffective. For example, although quite a number of young people had become homeless in the course of the study very few were homeless at the end of it. Similar efforts were required to keep young people in further education, although dropout rates were high and support seemed less successful. Very little attention seemed to be focused on relationships with the young persons' families.

One of the intentions of the Leaving Care Act was to introduce some standardi-sation across leaving care services. Given this was a national policy, a comparison with young people receiving no support was impossible. Care leavers in all authori-ties were entitled to support. This study therefore could not generate information on relative cost-effectiveness. Instead, statistical analysis was used to explore the extent to which the costs of support were associated with the young people's needs and their changes in welfare (outcomes) nine or ten months later.[5] Three variables were significantly associated with costs. Each additional placements move prior to receiving leaving care support was associated with an extra cost of £37 per week. Young people who thought they had weaker family support cost an extra £86 per week compared to those with fair or strong family support. Those perceived by the workers to have mental health problems cost an extra £81 per week compared to those who did not. However, even a combination of these needs and characteristics explained only 17 per cent of the variation in costs. We do not know if the remain-ing variation was random or due to factors not collected in the study.

This study clearly illustrates the role of wider policies in the outcomes achieved and the importance of inter-agency collaboration. The provision of housing depended on local policies as well as the availability of housing options. So did the delivery of further education. Low eligibility rates for social security benefits left many young people in need of additional financial support. Young people were obviously less likely to obtain jobs if these were in short supply. Arguably the

---

5   This type of cost function analysis would take the study closer to a cost consequences analysis in which the associations between cost and several outcomes are examined (see Chapter 4).

outcomes also depended on policies elsewhere within the social service departments. Examples are the poor outcomes of 'early discharges' and the lack of opportunity for young people to stay on with their foster carers for any extended lengths of time.

Local authorities now have a legal duty to provide leaving care services. While it is unlikely that prior to 2001 authorities spent no money on care leavers, it is likely that since then they are spending more. Figure 4.1 in shows that leaving care services absorb 5 per cent of social services expenditure. In 1994–5, the figure was just 1 per cent. On average, the total support cost for a care leaver in this study was just over £400 per week (including an average of £20 per week for the care leaver teams' input) of which nearly three-quarters was funded by social services for accommodation and other support. If as a result of such services fewer care leavers are homeless in the longer term, and fewer are unemployed or involved in crime, then social care services' investment today will 'pay off' in terms of user benefits and cost savings to the public purse in the future. The case is as yet unproven.

So what on balance can be said for the leaving care services? They are well appreciated and used. They support one of the most 'needy' of groups who are likely to find transition to adult life very difficult. As so often happens, young people with more severe difficulties appeared to be getting more support (as we should expect), but were still those with worse outcomes. These services are, however, almost certainly responsible for preventing some deterioration and, in particular, appear to prevent homelessness. Like other services they have to be evaluated in their context and against the objectives that it is reasonable to set them.

Services for looked after children

Earlier overviews have considered the two main components of the care system: residential care and foster care. These suggest a number of generalisations.

- There are major differences in the effects of different residential homes and different foster families, with residential homes in particular varying from the benign and homely to hotbeds of bullying and criminality.

- These differences relate in part to the characteristics of the carers, staff and, particularly, the managers of homes.

- In both foster care and residential care there are 'spirals of interaction'. One difficulty can easily spark off another leading to a breakdown of relationships and negative outcomes.

- There are serious problems in ensuring that any positive effects of either foster or residential care are 'carried over' to the child or young person's subsequent career.

- Much is known about the essential ingredients of successful support for foster families.
- Something is known about the likely requirements for the successful support of children's homes.

The three relevant studies in the initiative support and build on these generalisations. None of these are designed in a way that allows us to assess the relative effectiveness, or the cost-effectiveness, of these services against others. This was not their intention. But again, each contains information that may identify some courses of action as more reasonable than others.

Adoption study

The Adoption study had much to say on foster care and adoption as well as on the children's lives before they were looked after. Like other research, this emphasised the crucial role of children's wishes and of other children in making or breaking the placement. Again like others the researchers emphasised the impact on the placement of the child's behaviour, the need to provide accurate information to carers at the beginning of a placement and the nature and value of social work support. They also added new insights – on the key role of fathers, particularly for children who initially refused to relate to women – and on the degree to which in the carers' eyes a child's attachment could compensate for their behaviour.

Like studies in previous overviews the adoption study found little difference between the shorter-term outcomes of foster care and adoption. Foster carers were, however, very critical of their lack of parental authority and of the pressure on the young people to leave home before, in the carers' view, they were ready. These long-term foster carers believed the children were not as closely attached to them as the adoptive parents did. Problems around parental authority and long-term security may explain why this was so.[6] It was certainly the case that the few children who had left foster care were not doing very well.

Although the adopted sample fared in certain respects better than the others they were certainly not free of problems. At follow-up 44 per cent of the children had problems in three or more areas (for example, learning difficulties, attachment or emotional and conduct problems). The extent of these problems varied over the child's career with a child who was free of problems at one time being liable to develop them at another. In response to these problems the adoptive parents had sought help. This had involved them in contacts with a wide range of professionals.

---

6   It should be noted, however, that delays in decision-making about permanent placements were more likely in the case of fostered children. These delays may have made it more difficult for the children to attach to their carers.

Many of these contacts, however, were brief. For example, although more than half had seen a CAMHS professional, only 16 per cent of those referred to CAMHS had received treatment. In general the adopters saw these contacts as too little and too late. A third were indeed happy with their level of contact but a third wanted advice and a further third wanted more substantial intervention.

This powerful study is, in many ways, better seen as providing an analytic description of services than an evaluation of them. The early histories and characteristics of those adopted, stably fostered and unstably looked after were not the same. It cannot therefore be assumed that any differences in outcome were related to service characteristics. That said, the evidence, like that of some other studies, does suggest that the outcomes of adoption may have been marginally better than those of long-term foster care. A major difference occurs at 16 and over. At this point the fostered child is encouraged to think of leaving care schemes and grants. The adopted child is more likely to be envisaging an ongoing family life, speculating perhaps about university and concentrating on GCSEs.

As the authors point out, the implications are partly for assessment. We have discussed these earlier. They also bear on the need for improved adoption support. Finally they may have implications for long-term foster care. This may need to become more like adoption, something that is not necessarily truncated at the age of 16 or 17 and in which the carers have more of the authority commonly exercised by ordinary parents. At present the system is in danger of squandering both the financial investment in these placements and the emotional capital. Much has been spent on finding and maintaining an appropriate placement. In fortunate cases love has grown on both sides. All this is in danger of being forgone.

Foster Carer study

The Foster Carer study focused on issues related to remuneration in foster care. It began by using published statistics to explore variations between local authorities in measures of performance related to foster care (see Chapter 4). The researchers then used focus groups and a large postal survey of 2000 carers to examine the issues in 16 local authorities, selected to illustrate different patterns of expenditure and performance, and five independent fostering agencies.

The female carers[7] in this survey were overwhelmingly white (95%), married (70%) and aged between 36 and 55 (72%). About one-third went out to work. Older carers (about 18% were over 55) played an important role. As the study

---

7   The researchers tend to report figures for female carers only. They do not give the proportion of male carers but this is almost certainly very low.

points out, these carers are coming to the end of their fostering career and their departure will have implications for recruitment.

Although very few of these carers were in it 'for the money', they often relied on the income it brought. Their income from other sources was generally less than £20,000 per year. For this reason, and because most (61%) thought fostering should be salaried, money was important. Most were dissatisfied with the level of payment. There was also widespread dissatisfaction with the details of payment, for example with the bureaucracy surrounding incidental expenditure, the lack of retainers and the situation over tax. Finance had a particular impact on adoption. About three in eight foster carers had considered adopting but only one in eight had done so. As reported in an earlier overview many were dissuaded from doing so by the perceived drop in financial and other support.

There were considerable variations in the support that foster carers received. Carers working for independent fostering agencies generally received more support and reported greater satisfaction with this. Among local authorities the mean caseloads for supervising social workers ranged between 7 and 22 foster carers while the corresponding range for the independent fostering agencies was from 4 to 11. Carers were also more satisfied where they had regular monthly visits of at least an hour from their supervising social worker, where all their fostered children had been allocated a social worker, where they always received care plans and where they had their review on time. Satisfied carers were also more likely to take part in training, foster carer groups and social events and to feel part of a team and valued.

Overall the study amply illustrates the importance of payment, payment level and the way it is administered in the motivations behind foster caring. It was noticeable, however, that when given a choice only one in five foster carers favoured higher payments if that meant supervising social worker contact and other supports from the organisation would be reduced, and just over half of the carers rejected this proposal. In these ways the study helps address knotty issues around how payment, remuneration and other supports can help recruitment and retention – both of which are surely relevant to the outcomes for looked after children.[8] The study also shows that remuneration on its own is only a partial answer to the problem of recruiting and supporting carers. There are easier ways than foster care of earning a living. Those who foster generally do so for altruistic reasons and they want to feel valued and part of a team.

---

8   It is important to disentangle notions of payment, professionalism and love. It is sometimes assumed that those who are paid care less and that professionalism requires a lack of emotional involvement. There is no evidence that in the context of foster care these generalisations apply or that it would be appropriate if they did.

Children's Home study

The Children's Home study built on evidence from earlier studies suggesting that managers of children's homes had a major influence on their performance. It aimed to discover what it was that effective homes managers did, how this related to resources, and how what was done achieved a reasonable environment in the home or longer-term change in the residents.

Forty-five homes were involved in the study, 15 from the independent sector and 30 from eight local authorities. The researchers collected data using postal questionnaires to finance departments, homes' managers, residential staff and social workers. The young people living in the homes completed questionnaires twice, approximately a year apart. The researchers combined this quantitative information with a more detailed qualitative study of the managers' approach gained through telephone interviews, and discussions with staff groups in a sub-sample of ten homes.

Like previous studies in this area this research documented differences in the behaviour and well-being of residents in the different homes. These were far larger than could be explained by differences in the characteristics of the young people. They were, however, related to the role played by the manager of the home. As the researchers report, one variable dominated. In homes where the manager had clear, well worked-out strategies for dealing with behaviour and education, staff were found to have higher morale. They felt that they received clearer and better guidance, and that the children behaved better. Young people were less likely to be excluded from school and were less likely to be convicted or cautioned while living in the home. They also expressed more favourable views about the social climate of the home, were happier on some research measures, and their social workers felt they were functioning better.

Clear strategies were, it seemed, more likely to exist where the managers had a clear, sanctioned management role and a relatively high degree of autonomy. Such managers were also more likely to see themselves as the leader of a team whose practice they influenced and to ensure that their strategies were enshrined in guidance, induction and so on.

The study does not compare children's homes with other forms of provision such as foster care. It therefore cannot say whether taken as a whole these homes are more, or less, effective or cost-effective than other provisions. It did, however, identify several factors that taken together were associated with higher weekly costs per child.[9] One of these factors was that children who had been in the home longer tended to have lower unit costs per week.[10] Moreover, improved well-being was associated with longer length of stay, after allowing for a measure of environmental pressure to commit offences prior to entry to the home, and the sector of home.[11] More important was what the study did not find. After allowing for differences between children at intake, there was no evidence that the major differences in behaviour and well-being between homes were associated with either costs or the staffing ratios (to which costs are closely related).

The new evidence brought by this study is important. It suggests, as others have done, that the role of the manager is crucial in developing the ethos of the home. But it goes beyond other studies. It identifies the key characteristics of this leadership role and the organisational characteristics that facilitate it. Differences in the behaviour and roles of the managers seemed to account for the fact that independent homes in the study appeared to function better than the local authority ones.[12] Of course, we cannot generalise from this and say unequivocally that the independent sector is more effective than the local authorities.[13] However, it is clear that there are ways that some managers work that provide pointers to better practice in other homes.

So what, on balance, does the study have to say about residential care homes? Clearly this form of provision is targeted on a very complex group, some of whom, on other evidence, may well prefer it. As with other studies, the average outcomes are, at first sight, dispiriting. There is little evidence in this report that many of the homes have a highly developed rationale (see also the Troubled Adolescent study).

---

9   The multiple regressions tested simultaneously for associations using a range of characteristics and needs. Length of stay, pressure to temptation before admission to the home and location in the south of England were also associated with the unit cost per week of the home plus external services.

10 Although of course as time passes and the young person spends more weeks in the home so costs will accumulate.

11 Young people with many placements are commonly more disturbed than others and are likely to stay in any one place for a shorter time. There could be selection effects so that unhappy young people tend to leave the homes early leaving a residue of more contented residents who stay longer. Alternatively residents could become happier as they rise in 'seniority' in the home and become less vulnerable to bullying and more reconciled to their lot. It is also possible that the homes sort out the problems of longer-staying residents in some more fundamental way.

12 The finding has methodological interest. It could be argued that it is easier to provide effective leadership in homes, where, for whatever reason, the children's well-being is high. The chain of cause and effect could therefore flow in the opposite direction. However it is unlikely that the 'well-being' of residents influences the sector in which the home is located. So the evidence that sector (independent or local authority) is related to outcomes through the presence of leadership strategies is evidence that the causal chain stems, at least partly, from the way the manager of the home exercises their role.

13 In order to do this we would need to be sure that the independent and local authority homes were both representative of their sectors. The study cannot give this guarantee.

There is, however, abundant evidence that homes differ greatly in the well-being of their residents in ways that are not explained by the characteristics of the residents themselves. In the short run at least some homes seem to be much more effective than others and this has much more to do with the way they are managed than with the money that is spent on them.

In general, consumer demand, the sheer difficulty of containing some adolescents in foster care, and the need to provide some brief 'holding' centres are likely to lead to the continued existence of some residential care homes. What then might be done to improve the average level of their performance? There is a belief among staff that poorer outcomes reflect inadequate staffing levels. Staff members were also more likely to believe that staffing levels were too low where the outcomes measured were poorer.[14] By contrast there were no associations between outcomes and the actual staff to resident staffing ratios. On the evidence of this study attempts to improve the quality of residential care should rely more on the quality of staff, particularly the manager of the home, rather than just the numbers of staff in post.

Conclusion

The studies did not set out to assess the overall effectiveness of particular services, and can say little about it. They do, however, suggest ways forward or identify some courses of action that are more reasonable than others.

First the studies make clear the vital role of the social workers' assessments, widely construed as including the collection of information over time. As the adoption study showed, these assessments can be wrong. This is inevitable. Risks have to be run. The adoption study was only concerned with decisions to keep children in the community if these had gone wrong. It could not highlight the successes. That said, hindsight showed that much did go very wrong. Attempts to minimise these mistakes are likely to rely partly on procedures (such as arrange-

---

14   It is possible to reconcile staff views with the statistical findings. A high staff ratio may not prevent trouble. If it did one would expect to find that homes with more generous staffing levels had less trouble. Nevertheless, trouble occurring for reasons that have nothing to do with the level of staffing may require more generous staffing levels – for example, to respond to the need for one member of staff to take a young person to hospital after they have cut their wrists while another remains to supervise the home. Such incidents are not routine but occur more frequently in some homes than others, leaving their staff complaining of insufficient staffing. Anecdotal evidence suggests that some homes respond to domestic disturbances by calling on the police to quell disturbances, an understandable strategy that tends to lead to charges and the further criminalisation of young people. This line of argument suggests a need to respond to difficulties by temporary increases in staffing or the ability to supply staff quickly in an emergency rather than a need to provide a high level of staffing on a continuous basis. At present children's homes may be staffed with a view not to what occurs on a routine basis but with an eye to what might occur.

ments which insist on parallel planning or on a review of decisions within an agreed timescale). They may also rely on organisational arrangements such as those outlined in the Assessment Framework study and on clear agreed protocols for making referrals for other specialist assessments. In the end, however, they depend essentially on the skill of the social workers and, as argued next, on the resources available to them.

Second, decisions over keeping a child in the community need to be made in a context of adequate community resources, both those within social services and those from other agencies and organisations. The Adoption study was critical of the degree to which the supports for families were either inadequate or temporarily adequate and then suddenly reduced when the family appeared to respond so that the family again relapsed. In this sense there was a disparity between the over-riding desire to keep children with their families and the level of resources devoted to this end. So there is a case, as earlier overviews have argued, for increasing the resources devoted to those who are supported in their families.

The Care Leaver study exemplified one strategy for community services. The care leaving teams did not attempt radical improvements in, for example, a young person's relationship with their family. They did, however, respond vigorously and apparently successfully to crises of homelessness. This strategy contrasted with that pursued by the specialist adolescent support teams. Here the teams did attempt to change behaviour and family relationships. These relationships did improve, arguably but not definitely because of the teams' efforts. The adolescent support teams were certainly popular with their users, and probably increased the number of families served. They also demonstrated the viability of a strategy that, while not denying the value of short-term care, avoids the dichotomy between unwelcome long-term care for adolescents and no service at all. This strategy may achieve change or simply allow it to occur. Either way it is worth serious consideration.

Third, the studies do make the case for some refocusing of resources. Suggestions that can be made include the following.

- Good quality assessments can benefit the children's care career and the costs are low compared to the potential costs of subsequent support. It therefore seems unwise to reduce the level of resources devoted to assessment as a means of saving money.

- Adolescent support teams seemed more popular with their users than mainstream services, no more costly, at least as effective on other grounds and more likely to prevent admission to long-term care. They were mainly staffed by former residential workers and at least partly funded by the closure of the homes in which team members had worked. This strategy for redistributing resources should be considered.

- Support is very important to formal carers and should enhance carer retention and recruitment.[15] The provision of additional resources for carer support may well help increase the pool of foster carers allowing a subsequent reduction in dependence on the more expensive residential care placements.

Fourth, the Adoption Study in particular supports the case for looking again at long-term fostering. As argued in the most recent of the research overviews, *Fostering Now* (Sinclair 2005), some children are not going to be adopted but are equally unable to return home. For others the only chance of adoption is with their foster carers. So there is a need to look at the points raised in the Adoption study. Given that some carers are effectively parenting their foster children does this role need additional recognition?[16] Is it appropriate that the common assumption should be that the children do not stay on beyond 18?[17] As the Foster Carer study asks, should the financial and other disincentives associated with foster carer adoptions be removed?[18]

Fifth, the studies demonstrate that results depend not only on resources but also on good practice. Foster carers require adequate remuneration. They also need to be valued as members of a team, something that is more likely to be ensured by good practice than higher expenditure. Appropriate decisiveness in adoption is not ensured by finance. It probably costs, in the end, less than indecision. While staff believed that more resources were essential to the success of children's homes there was no evidence that those with higher staff ratios did better. By contrast there was ample evidence of the crucial impact of the strategies of the manager of the home.

A minimum implication of the importance of good practice is that it is vital to monitor the quality of placements. Curiously the study of Troubled Adolescents found that this was not always done. Authorities appeared to use a wide range of single, external placements without apparently having a clear strategic plan for

---

15   Much recruitment is by word of mouth so that contented carers are likely to be effective recruiters.

16   Examples of steps that might be taken include the insistence that such arrangements are always sanctioned by a panel and do not arise 'de facto' and the delegation of more powers of decision-making to foster carers as suggested in the Adoption and Foster Carer studies. Greater clarity about the long-term status of some foster children may provide scope for negotiation on price with independent agencies that may be persuaded to respond to the greater certainty of an agreed long-term placement with a reduction in fees.

17   The Care Leaver study did find some children staying beyond 18. However, this seemed to be a brief arrangement while things were sorted out, a finding in keeping with those of studies in the *Fostering Overview* (Sinclair 2005).

18   The Adoption Act 2002 has extended the possibilities for long-term care. This includes the concept of special guardianship to complement adoption, residence orders and long-term foster care. The *Fostering Review* argues that there needs to be 'a level playing field' between these different forms of provision so that foster carers are not dissuaded from taking up these options for fears of financial hardship, inability to provide properly for the foster child or loss of support.

how these placements were chosen, an institutional memory of what they were like, nor clear rules for how the children's progress and safety were monitored. Gaps in files made it difficult for new workers taking over, while managers apparently had no overview of the pattern of placements that were used. Lack of such information must make it difficult for managers to assess the quality of the provision they use and thus to use opportunities offered by the 'market' to drive up quality.

Some of the suggestions arising from the studies will require quite high levels of extra resources. This would be true, for example, for the provision of further adoption support or for arrangements to enable young people to stay on in foster care beyond 18. For others, resources are already in place and it is the way they are used that requires careful consideration. Resources are already allocated to training under the new workforce initiative. So it is a question of ensuring that these resources are used to transmit the relevant skills, and that those skills are used. Some suggestions require greater collaboration with others. Under *Every Child Matters* organisational arrangements will soon be in place nationally to encourage and facilitate inter-agency processes and strategies.

So there are four strands that have to be in place – good practice, adequate resources, appropriate use of resources and appropriate policies. The identification of what is good or appropriate depends in part, although only in part, on research. Our final chapter considers what this initiative can say about practice, resources, policies and research.

Summary

This chapter focuses on services for children on the verge of the care system or recently or currently in it. Taken together the studies covered assessment and planning, preventive work with adolescents, adoption, foster care, residential care, and the work of leaving care teams.

Studies of assessment and care planning showed that these could be difficult and time consuming. Nevertheless they could bear fruit in terms of better joint working between agencies and better partnerships with parents. By contrast poor assessment and planning could lead to delay in adoption decisions – which may impact on the likelihood of the child being adopted and lead to high care costs over time – and to children who are already using expensive services not receiving relatively inexpensive but badly needed help. Investment in assessment and care planning costs little in comparison with the costs of poor decisions over children's care. One general implication of the studies was that a very high priority should be given to this aspect of practice.

Other suggestions put forward relate to:

- the provision of resources adequate for providing community support for families of young children on the verge of entering the care system
- the development of adolescent prevention teams that are likely to be a cost-effective service for some teenagers, are popular with families and may reduce the use of the care system
- removal of financial disincentives to carer adoptions
- the development of a framework for 'permanent fostering'
- better remuneration for foster carers, more efficient means for dealing with financial issues for carers and a continued recognition of their other needs for support
- the possible scope for reducing the cost of residential care where good leadership was associated with better immediate outcomes but higher staffing ratios and costs were not
- a better 'institutional memory' of what placements are like that will help managers use opportunities offered by the market to drive up quality
- the continued development of the care leaving teams as a 'fire-fighting' service for crises such as homelessness
- continued attention to the 'strategic needs' of care leavers in terms, for example, of their need for good housing, good opportunities for further education and, in some cases, the chance to stay on with their foster carers.

These suggestions depend variously on changes in policies, the provision of resources, the use of resources and practice. Above all they point to the paramount importance of the quality of practice and placements in the care system.

Chapter 7

Conclusion

Introduction

The services studied in this initiative pre-dated the proposals set out in *Every Child Matters*. There is now a new vision of child welfare. The aim is to promote services such that every child is enabled to fulfil their potential; services are delivered at an early point and in an integrated way; professionals look at the whole child and refer to others as appropriate; everyone is focused on improving outcomes for children and no child falls between the service net.

This new vision encompasses five rather different kinds of strategies.

1. Broad national initiatives intended to tackle poverty, poor housing and other sources of deprivation and inequality.

2. Initiatives targeted at deprived communities but designed in particular to improve the lives of the children in them.

3. Services designed to assist families at an early stage of difficulty.

4. Specialist services designed to resolve specific problems affecting children.

5. Services that are intended for children for whom the state has taken responsibility or for whom this is a serious possibility.

This research initiative covered only the last three of these. Within this context five questions arise. These relate to:

1. *Evidence*
   Is the evidence strong enough to form a basis for policy or do we need to strengthen it?

2. *Prevention*
   Can services not traditionally provided by social services department prevent the problems on which these departments have concentrated and thus save money or use the same money to better effect?

3.   *Early intervention*
     What does the evidence suggest are the most fruitful areas for earlier intervention?

4.   *Later intervention*
     What does the evidence suggest about reconfiguring those services traditionally provided by social services departments so that they are more in keeping with the new vision?

5.   *Operating challenges*
     What are the operational challenges that need to be faced if this is to happen?

Improving the evidence

The initiative has fostered the development of children's social care research on costs and effectiveness of services in the UK. It has provided studies that use economic theory. They have estimated the time spent on certain activities, estimated unit costs and sought to disentangle the costs of social work and commissioning along with the costs incurred by different agencies in the service of the same children. The studies have also explored the effectiveness and cost-effectiveness of different kinds of provision, and the varying ways the same type of service (such as residential care) is provided, how it could be more effective, and its relative costs. In all these ways the initiative has helped to advance both knowledge in this field and the techniques used to obtain it.

Despite this advance uncertainties remain. These reflect the lack of repeated studies, the inevitable (if different) limitations of different research designs, the lack in most cases of an experimental test, the limited range of outcomes tested and the limited lengths of time over which users were followed up. In the longer term it is essential to improve the evidence. In the short term the task is to use the tools provided by researchers in local enquiries and to make the best judgements possible in the light of the available evidence. The central task of this conclusion is to discuss these 'best judgements'. Before doing this we should say something about the implications for research and for using the findings in local studies.

In the longer term research has to be cumulative. This means it must be informed by general ideas. The results from research can then modify these ideas and also gain plausibility from them.[1] Within this context we make seven suggestions:

---

1   A good example is provided by the approach adopted in the SPOKES project. This was partly informed by ideas on authoritative parenting and approaches to parent training. The largely positive results are more plausible because of this earlier work. The results also provide evidence in favour of the general approach. It could also be argued that interventions are more likely to produce lasting results if they are targeted at points when key relationships are being formed as in the specialist health visiting service.

1.   A continuing use of quasi-experimental and 'descriptive-analytic' studies. These are necessary to develop the ideas that need to be tested and, of equal importance, to see if apparently effective supports can be successfully implemented more widely.

2.   More experimental interventions that recruit an adequate number of 'subjects' and last for an adequate length of time.[2] In the end the only way of seeing whether a suggestion works is to try it out and see. Failure to do this risks not only a waste of money but also a waste of lives.[3]

3.   Use of a greater variety of research methods. Statistical techniques are needed to estimate effects. Descriptive and qualitative work is essential for defining the nature of interventions, assessing the plausibility of statistical conclusions, picking up unintended side effects, giving a voice to practitioners and service users and assessing the value of the intervention in the context of their lives.

4.   Greater attention to issues around diversity. Sensitive qualitative studies are needed to draw lessons from small groups along with more reviews that combine findings from different studies (see, for example, Thorburn, Chand and Procter 2005).

5.   Many more studies that include an economic perspective. Decisions are informed by considerations of cost. Without this perspective much research will fail to have an impact at all. Any research proposal in this field that does not include an economic component should make clear why this is so.

6.   More systematic research reviews that integrate the different kinds of research evidence needed. They cannot rely on simply counting, or in some sense averaging, the results of different randomised controlled trials.

7.   Local audits should make use of the tools developed in these studies for costing activities and for recording the different elements of service packages. The resulting information should not dominate the decisions of managers and social workers but should inform them.

---

2   These studies are very costly and can raise practical and ethical difficulties. A social work intervention is not a standard pill that is constant across a variety of settings. To facilitate replication, particular efforts are needed to understand the way an intervention works.

3   A poignant example is the decay of the practice of long-term support pioneered during the last world war by Family Services Units. No one knows how much this devoted work may have contributed to the welfare of children and their families. The approach has simply gone out of fashion.

Economics and children's social care

All research should start from the premise that an economic perspective will be *included*. There may be very good reasons for then *excluding* it, but if only the estimation of costs is considered, and then as an 'add-on' to the main research, the discipline will remain under-developed. As a starting point, however, there is a very basic need to continue the work of this research initiative on service use and unit costs. Further research is urgently needed to develop our understanding of the associations between costs, needs, and outcomes. There are also many broader issues in the economics of child social care that studies in this initiative started to consider.

This general approach has implications for those funding the research and those who might participate in it. Research funders need to appreciate the value (and costs) of this kind of research and of the need to embed it in a programme. Services need to see research as central to their role. Almost all the researchers in this initiative reported on the very real difficulties they had in recruiting sites and samples.[4] These problems can only be addressed if account is taken of the costs to services and organisations of participating, and of the need to provide them with feedback tailored to their needs (itself something that requires investment).

Balancing prevention and later intervention

In Chapter 5 we defined 'early interventions' as those occurring before there is any serious consideration that a child might enter the care system. It is commonly hoped that these services will be 'preventive'. The argument is that money spent on them will reduce the need to spend money on later more intensive supports. How far does the evidence of this initiative support this argument?

In the short term the findings suggest that it is highly unlikely that the services not provided by social services would reduce social services costs or change their pattern of operation. Current expenditure on social care services is heavily concentrated on those who are already in very serious difficulty. On the whole, the children and families in contact with the specialist health visitors, the Home-Start

---

4   This was not because those who took part found the experience unpleasant. Many valued the opportunity to have their voice heard. But many also commented that they were concerned that little happens as a result of their input. Pressure of work, inspections, special measures, organisational changes, all played their part in making authorities reluctant to participate and social workers reluctant to identify children and families.

volunteers or the services offering treatment for sexual abuse faced very serious problems. Nevertheless these difficulties were not likely to result in an admission to care. So expenditure on the 'high cost' social care group today will probably not be reduced by use of those services. Indeed such services may well have the effect of increasing awareness of risk, and hence increasing pressures on the care system. The specialist health visitor service provided evidence that this was indeed the case. Whilst in the long run preventive intervention may well lead to improvements in the life chances of children it will not lead to financial savings in the short term. For this reason a shift towards these preventive services must either come from 'new money' or depend on economies in current services.

In the longer term, each of these services may have an impact on reducing referrals of children and young people to social services – we do not as yet know. Using overarching findings from the studies we can identify three challenges for prevention services:

1. Services must reach populations at risk. Some of the services studied were almost certainly not contacting a high proportion of those at risk. The Home-Start service seemed to be dealing with a population that was, for social care services, low risk. The specialist health visitor,[5] therapeutic family support service and sexual abuse services seem to have contacted low proportions of those at risk, and in two cases at a late stage. Perhaps, the most successful intervention in terms of reaching its target population was the SPOKES project. Six out of ten of the parents were willing to reply to the questionnaire that introduced this project but it is not known how far those who did not reply were either without difficulties or particularly burdened by them.

2. The services when taken together should meet the needs of the population served. These needs are likely to be wide and varied, and the services studied here are clearly not comprehensive in terms of meeting all relevant needs either on their own or in combination with the others. None of them, for example, set out their stall to deal with drug addiction, adult mental health or learning difficulties. None specifically dealt with domestic abuse, although some probably dealt with it by referral and discussion. The SPOKES workers focused on child behaviour and reading – it is doubtful how far their service would have been able to handle serious family problems, or would even have been aware of them. The general picture of both the Home-Start and family

---

5   The midwives referred 433 women of whom 120 refused to see the researcher, 150 were seen as unsuitable for the study by the researcher and a further 31 dropped out after this point. These figures are obviously influenced by the fact that recruitment was not simply to an intervention but rather to a randomised controlled trial. Further research would be needed to establish recruitment rates to this intervention if offered in usual practice.

support interventions were that they dealt with only some aspects of a range of difficulties. In the case of Home-Start the women involved generally solved other difficulties on their own. In the case of the family support services the problems were more serious and often proved intractable.

Arguably the project best placed to provide or enable a comprehensive service was the specialist health visiting service. Whereas this concentrated on specific issues (for example, mother baby interaction), it sought to do so in the context of a relationship between the mother and the health visitor within which key issues of concern were likely to be raised. This in turn should have allowed referral where this was necessary. In this way the service may have achieved the 'best of both worlds' – a service that had an adequate focus but was also able to ensure that other difficulties could be addressed if necessary.

3. Each service must be effective in dealing with the problems it addresses. Only three of the services studied (the SPOKES, specialised health visiting and sexual abuse studies) were able to provide even limited evidence of being more effective than the routine services used by the comparison groups of children and families.[6] Arguably the Home-Start service enabled users to get back on their feet quicker or to achieve certain specialised gains. It was not, however, designed to deal with many of the problems that these families faced. Offering support, friendship and practical assistance may not be enough for those struggling to manage on a low income, get proper services for a disabled child or free themselves from a violent husband.

Obviously the studies in this initiative could not cover all possible forms of prevention. We believe, however, that the interventions would be widely accepted as being as promising as any others. It is therefore important that overall the findings suggest that no single 'preventive' service is likely to achieve high, comprehensive and effective coverage of those at risk. The savings they produce for social care services will probably not be great and, if they transpire, will be some time in the future.

The case for early intervention lies in the improvement of outcomes for children and families rather than short-term service savings. It is likely to depend on the development and integration of a wide range of specific services. The longer-term case for prevention also has to be made on the basis of outcomes not cost savings – and if cost savings do result, they may well benefit other agencies rather than those offering prevention. In the immediate future a shift to preventive services will almost certainly cost money.

---

6   It is logically possible that the family support services were effective in preventing deterioration.

> ## Economy, efficiency and effectiveness
>
> This report is not about efficiency savings that are imposed by central government. Neither does it suggest that care services should do the same thing more cheaply. There is a need for a network of services, some responding to a wide range of need at an early point, some providing a more specialist service that can be assessed against specific outcomes, and some more intensive care for children whose situation would otherwise be intolerable. Within these different kinds of services, however, there are almost certainly ways to use the same resources to improve outcomes or to serve more users equally effectively.

Improving preventative services

If the case for early intervention depends on outcomes how far can it draw support from this initiative? Basically it strengthens the case for developing the specialist health visitor and SPOKES projects.

- Each of these appears to be more effective than routinely available services. In the case of the specialist Health Visitor study there is evidence that although it is more expensive, it may also be cost-effective.

- Both these interventions are linked to universal services (health visiting and school) and thus potentially able to serve all their intended clientele.

- Both were able to target and recruit families in recognisable difficulty.

- Both had a recognisable rationale and are supported by other evaluative work – specifically that associated with the work of D. Olds and of C. Webster-Stratton.[7]

- Arguably both were targeted at strategic points (birth and arrival at school) where small changes in relationships are more likely to have long-term and cumulative effects.

Both have the additional benefit that they may be able to identify those who are not likely to respond to this approach and who require something different or more intensive. In the case of early home visiting this may well not directly benefit

---

7   For some references see selected reading on parenting programmes, at the end of the References. The general conclusion seems to be that there is quite strong evidence in favour of these approaches, although reviewers differ in their assessment of the strength of this evidence. There is still doubt about the degree to which the effects last and the identification of those who will and will not respond.

children who are at high risk of abuse (MacMillan *et al.* 2005). It should, however, enable these children to be identified at a time when more intensive support or perhaps adoption, are still possible.

These services have not been conclusively evaluated.[8] They are not the only kinds of early interventions that are needed. They have, however, a stronger evidence base to inform development than is available for other services. The evidence is, on the whole, encouraging and this must provide one reason for considering their expansion.

Improving later interventions

Later interventions are focused on those who are, might be or have been looked after in the care system. Research in the initiative highlights some of the issues relevant to it. These concern:

- *Permanency*
  How far does the current system ensure that all children have a family base where they are safe and where they feel that they properly belong?

- *Community care*
  Is sufficient and appropriate support provided for children who are permanently based with their parents?

- *Corporate parenting*
  How far does the local authority provide the kind of parenting to those in its care that 'ordinary' parents would take for granted?

- *Views of young people and carers*
  To what extent are support services valued by recipients and users?

In assessing services against these criteria we will concentrate first on problems and then on pointers to development. Inevitably this approach concentrates more on new or innovative services rather than 'standard' ones. We should emphasise therefore that almost all the reports contain examples of high quality practice in 'ordinary' services. Thus 'ordinary' leaving care services appeared to respond effectively to the crisis of homelessness; 'ordinary' foster carers appreciated the support they received and were unwilling to sacrifice it to the increased financial rewards they also desired; different social services department responded creatively to the challenges posed by demands for 'care'. Examples of this kind could easily be multiplied.

---

8   As argued earlier there is a need for longer follow-up and for evaluation in 'non-experimental' conditions.

That said, there was still room for improvement. Much of the care provided was impermanent. Long-term foster children in the Adoption study were not offered the kind of permanent base ordinary families usually give to their own children. Community-based care was good in places but often patchy. The Assessment Framework study, the Adoption study and, at a different end of the age range, the Adolescent Prevention study, all suggested that care was 'all or nothing' – provision for those who were not looked after was often short-term, inadequate or non-existent. The Adoption study and the Care Careers study both showed that young people often attracted immensely expensive provision without any consideration being paid to quite simple needs – for example, a difficulty in reading.

What is required if these problems are to be tackled?

First, more resources have to be devoted to those currently served by social care services in the community. In common with earlier initiatives this one highlighted the drastic rationing that takes place when children are referred. The Assessment Framework study suggested that many of the children whose cases were closed after initial assessment had high levels of need. If these children are to receive adequate supports, additional resources will have to be devoted to them.

Additional community resources may also be required in order to:

- provide an adequate service to children returned home 'on trial' that is, one that lasts as long as needed and is as intensive as needed

- develop specialist adolescent support teams for teenagers who are having a lot of trouble living at home. These teams seemed on average to cost no more than routine ways of handling this group, to be much better accepted by their users and to lessen the chances of entry into the care system on a long-term basis.[9,10]

Second, decisions about individual cases have to improve. The studies highlighted the consequences that flowed, for example, from returning children home rather than placing children for adoption or from placing adolescents in homes that are not functioning well. Anything that can be done to improve decisions in these cases is likely to be money well spent.

In the third place there would be advantages to blurring the lines between the care system and 'community-based care'. This could involve, for example:

---

9   The apparent effect on long-term care was true of this study. If this effect turns out to hold good in a larger sample of authorities it would be expected to have an increasing impact in reducing costs as children in long-term care can accumulate high costs over time, particularly if they use residential care.

10   The National Service Framework for Mental Health recommends a number of different types of community-based teams, each with different roles for different groups of service users (crisis resolution, assertive outreach, early intervention, and so on). A benefit of this greater variety is likely to be a greater specificity of function, something that would be likely to make managing the service easier and to develop and concentrate the expertise with which it was delivered.

- Brief admissions – the study of adolescents suggested that the aim of adolescent support teams should be to reduce use of 'long-term' care rather than to prevent any admissions – something the evidence suggested was possible. Brief 'cooling off' admissions were seen as helpful.

- Treatment foster care – the Care Careers study suggested that young people who do not return home quickly are unlikely to experience a form of care designed to enable them to take control of their own behaviour and return home within a planned space of time. American models of treatment foster care may be worth exploring (see, for example, Leve and Chamberlain 2005).

Turning to those who cannot be supported in the community there are ways to encourage a slight increase in the number of children who are adopted. Improved assessment and improved monitoring of the consequences of assessment seem to be essential as are methods for hastening adoptions (such as parallel planning) when attempts at rehabilitation fail. As the Adoption study pointed out, failure to make appropriate assessments or to review the consequences of previous assessments can result in children losing the chance of adoption, in massive later costs and blighted lives. In addition there may be scope for increasing the number who are adopted by foster carers. As the Foster Carer study points out, many foster carers have thought of adoption but are dissuaded by concerns about the loss of finance or support. Extra carer support may help better decision-making about care for some children.

Finally there are children who cannot be adopted or supported in their own family. Over the age of five many children have lost the chance of adoption but remain in the care system. As shown in the Leaving Care study, leaving care teams achieved some success in supporting these young people on a 'crisis management' basis. Nevertheless, there is a case, powerfully made in the Adoption study, for enabling some of them to remain on with their carers after the age of 18. Such a policy would have consequences for the kind of parenting they receive earlier. Long-term foster carers perform a quasi-parental role for many foster children but lack parental authority (for example, over decisions on school trips). Special guardianship and adoption provide a 'solution' to this problem but it is likely that foster carers will be deterred from taking up these options by the same disincentives that dissuade them from adoption. Attention to those disincentives should again allow decisions about children to be taken on the basis of meeting the particular needs of those concerned rather than financial expediency.

These suggested changes would cost money. Only those concerned with adoption may actually save it and then only in the long run and to a limited extent, because finding and supporting adoptive placements is not cheap. Money is needed to:

- ensure more adequate community services for those 'at risk' of entering the care system

- recruit carers, retain them and respond to the pressures to enhance their remuneration and support packages

- finance the finding and support of adoptive families

- provide additional support for friends and family carers

- develop more specialist foster care

- enable more young people to stay on with their carers beyond 18.

Is there any scope for redistributing resources? Almost certainly there is some. One possibility is provided by residential care. Residential care, particularly units that provide for only one or two children, is extremely expensive. There are major variations in both the costs of different residential units and the well-being of those in them. Higher costs or higher staffing ratios in residential homes are not an effective way of 'buying' good performance.[11] In contrast good practice, particularly in the form of good leadership, appears essential to improving the care environment. Given the large variation in the costs of different residential homes there may be scope for savings in this area as practice improves or, perhaps, for using some heavily supported foster care in its stead.[12]

Overall what is being suggested is that authorities seek to gain a clear view of what proportions of their total spending are taken up by which of their clientele, review this picture, and consider seeking a more rational and equitable distribution.

Facing the operating challenges

The suggestions made in the last two sections will only work given three conditions:

1. appropriate assessment and care planning

2. timely and appropriate collaboration between services

3. availability of a range of high quality supports and services.

As in the discussion of 'later interventions' we will concentrate on problems and then promising ways forward. Again there is evidence of much good practice in ordinary services. For example, some mothers would not consider accessing the

---

11   Arguably they should be. There is no evidence that, for example, successful managers of homes are paid more than others. This may not be rational in a system that depends so heavily on the quality of staff.

12   The evidence for this is discussed in the latest 'messages for research' overview, *Fostering Now* (Sinclair 2005).

specialist health visiting service because they were reluctant to lose their own health visitor. In the Framework Assessment study the researchers saw some assessment as high class. Foster carers in the Adoption study varied in the quality of their care, and there were major variations in the quality and impact of children's homes.

We have argued above that assessment and care planning are part of a process. They depend on the accumulation of evidence, the careful monitoring of decisions, the existence of appropriate procedures and the availability of appropriate resources. They also depend on the ability of social workers not only to gather and weigh evidence but also to explore and negotiate solutions with their clients, their own managers and other services. All this takes time and money. We have argued above that these areas of work have to be a priority. If social workers do not assess their clients' situations, strengths and weaknesses their plans will be the poorer. Assessment that is not associated with appropriate plans is in vain.

In relation to collaboration there was, in general, goodwill but plenty of evidence of misunderstanding, failures to refer and inappropriate referral. Across all studies, collaboration was found to be patchy at best. Some of the difficulties did not involve resources; they arose from factors such as lack of a common 'language', misunderstanding of the roles of others, lack of common boundaries and difficulties in reaching clinic-based services. To these issues researchers suggested helpful solutions to implement better integration of processes – for example, the provision of joint training, work on common referral forms and so on. These difficulties will take an investment of staff time to resolve. Time costs money, but these solutions do not in themselves require a heavy investment of new money.

Another source of difficulty was almost certainly lack of staff and hence time. Collaboration will not create resources. Much of it is likely to increase demands for support. So the 'defensiveness' and 'restricted views of their service role' to which researchers have drawn attention may simply reflect a need to husband scarce time. This may explain the difficulties social workers had in returning calls; the waiting lists, specialised system of referral and restrictive criteria that characterised the CAMH service or the belief among many health visitors that their usual way of working only gave them time to provide a crisis service.

If collaboration is not 'free' it needs to be appropriate. One possible area for this relates to the sharing of expertise. All services seem to be drawing from the general pool of ideas. For example, ideas from social learning theory appear to be used to some extent in adolescent prevention teams, EBD schools and some family centres. At the same time the extent to which staff are trained in these ideas is very varied. Clinical psychologists are likely to have much greater training in cognitive and behavioural therapy (CBT) than social workers. According to the Child Protection study CAMH services often respond tardily or not at all to the clients referred by social workers. Psychologists might well spend more time in training and providing consultation to other professionals rather than in supplying direct services themselves.

Finally the initiative underlines the almost overwhelming importance of quality of provision. If a choice has to be made, it is improvements in quality rather structural change that hold the key to improvements in outcome. At present many, but not all, foster carers are caring, committed and clear in their expectations. Some social workers find it easier than others to communicate with children, weigh evidence or take balanced decisions. Some children's homes are benign. Others have a culture marked by delinquency, bullying and misery.

These considerations obviously bear on workforce planning, registration and inspection. Unfortunately, however, evidence on what counts as good care is not the same as evidence on how to bring it about. In theory training, support and appropriate organisation should all play a part in ensuring that individuals perform at their best. But not all training is the same and we need better evidence about what training is needed in what circumstances. Similarly we need to know what forms of support and organisation work best. Overall we do not yet have the evidence needed to inform development. Only the Children's Home study identified some of the conditions that seemed to promote high quality care. The task of understanding and promoting such quality provides crucial unfinished business for practitioners, researchers and policy-makers alike.

Conclusion

This book is based on research that antedated *Every Child Matters* but it does provide evidence to inform the development of services as now envisaged. Our suggestions include:

- steps to improve the evidence base while making the best use of the evidence available
- a recognition that the case for earlier interventions is more easily based on arguments about outcome, than arguments about cost savings
- the commitment of new resources to interventions that are supported by evidence and targeted at strategic points – notably intensive health visiting and interventions around the time a child starts school
- the need to review the way social services' resources are currently spent with the aim of redistributing resources in the way research suggests may be more rational.

The success of these changes will depend on appropriate care planning and assessment, appropriate collaboration between services, and, above all, on higher quality provision. Given these conditions services may move gradually, realistically and with increasing certainty towards the vision that *Every Child Matters* enshrines.

DfES Implementation and Advisory Group Members

Carolyn Davies	Chair of IAG and Costs and Effectiveness research programme manager
Celia Atherton	IAG lead and Director, Research in Practice
Ian Sinclair	Academic coordinator for the research programme and Research Professor, Social Work Research and Development Unit, University of York
Jennifer Beecham	Reader in Social Policy, Personal Social Services Research Unit, University of Kent
Cathy Ashley	Chief Executive, Family Rights Group
John Carpenter	Professor of Social Work and Applied Social Science, Centre for Health and Social Care, University of Bristol
Ross Cormick	Policy Assurance Manager, Children, Cheshire Social Services Department
Richard Cotmore	Senior Evaluation Officer, NSPCC
Colin Green	Divisional Manager, Safeguarding Children, DfES
Geraldine Macdonald	Director of Information and Knowledge Management, CSCI
John Rowlands	Professional Advisor, DfES
Rob Sinclair	Analyst/adviser on costs and effectiveness, Analytic Division, DfES
Meera Spillett	Deputy Director of Children's Services, Norfolk County Council
Robert Tapsfield	Chief Executive, Fostering Network
Andrew Webb	Director, Stockport Social Services Department
Caroline Thomas	Research Advisor and lead on the Quality Protects and Adoption research programmes, DfES
Consultative Groups	Parents and carers in Cheshire and Liverpool
	Young care leavers working with 'A National Voice'

Research Studies and Authors

1. The Oxfordshire Home Visiting Study

   J. Barlow, S. Stewart-Brown, H. Davis, E. Mackintosh, S. Kirkpatrick, P. Jarrett, C. Mockford

2. Child Care Costs: Variations and Unit Costs

   A. Bebbington and J. Beecham

3. Cost and Consequences of Services for Troubled Adolescents: An Exploratory, Analytic Study

   D. Berridge, J. Beecham, I. Brodie, T. Cole, H. Daniels, M. Knapp, V. MacNeill

4. The Costs and Effectiveness of Adolescent Support Teams

   N. Biehal, S. Byford, H. Weatherly

5. Outcomes and Costs of Therapeutic Family Support Services for Vulnerable Families with Young Children

   J. Carpenter, J. Tidmarsh, J. Slade, J. Schneider, P. Coolen-Schrijner, D. Wooff

6. The Assessment Framework: A Structured Approach to Assessing Family Capacities and Children's Needs

   H. Cleaver, S. Walker, P. Meadows

7. Young People Leaving Care: A Study of Costs and Outcomes

   J. Dixon, J. Wade, S. Byford, H. Weatherly, J. Lee

8. Leadership and Resources in Children's Homes

   L. Hicks, I. Gibbs, S. Byford, H. Weatherly

9. Meeting the Mental Health Needs of Children in the Child Protection System

   I. Katz, S. Bhabra, J. Corlyon, P. Moran, D. Ghate, V. La Placa, J. Beecham

10. Remuneration and Performance in Foster Care

    D. Kirton, J. Beecham, K. Ogilvie

11. Young Families under Stress: Outcomes and Costs of Home-Start Support

    C. McAuley, M. Knapp, J. Beecham, N. McCurry, M. Sleed
    (Funded by Joseph Rowntree Foundation)

12. Cost-effectiveness of Individual versus Group Psychotherapy for Sexually Abused Girls

    P. McCrone, T. Weeramanthri, M. Knapp, A. Rushton, J. Trowell, G. Miles, I. Kolvin

13. Cost and Outcomes of Non-infant Adoptions

    J. Selwyn, W. Sturgess, D. Quinton, C. Baxter

14. Cost and Consequences of Different Types of Child Care Provision

    H. Ward, L. Holmes, J. Soper, R. Olsen

References

Aldgate, J. and Statham, J. (2001) *The Children Act Now: Messages from Research.* London: HMSO.

Barclay, P.M. (1982) *Social Workers: Their Role and Tasks.* London: Bedford Square Press.

Beecham, J. (2000) *Unit Costs – Not Exactly Child's Play. A Guide to Estimating Unit Costs for Children's Social Care.* Dartington: Department of Health, Dartington Social Research Unit and PSSRU. Online at www.pssru.ac.uk/publications (accessed 5 May 2006).

Department for Education and Skills (DfES) (2001) *Children in Need Survey.* Online at www.dfes.gov.uk/qualityprotects/work-pro/analysis1.shtml (accessed 5 May 2006).

DfES (2003) *Children in Need Census 2003.* London: DfES. Online at www.dh.gov.uk/Publications AndStatistics/Statistics/StatisticalWorkAreas/StatisticalExpenditure/fs/en.

DfES (2004) *Every Child Matters: Change for Children.* Cm5860. London: DfES.

Department of Health (1985) *Social Work Decisions in Child Care.* London: HMSO.

Department of Health (1991) *Patterns and Outcomes in Child Placement: Messages for Current Research and the Implications.* London: HMSO.

Department of Health (1995) *Child Protection: Messages from Research.* London: HMSO.

Department of Health (1996) *Focus on Teenagers: Research into Practice.* London: HMSO.

Department of Health (1998) *Caring for Children Away from Home: Messages from Research.* Chichester: John Wiley & Sons.

Department of Health (2005) *Personal Social Services Expenditure and Unit Costs: England: 2003–2004.* London: HMSO. Online at www.dfes.gov.uk/datastats1/guidelines/children/children.shtml

Dretzke, J., Frew, E., Davenport, C., Barlow, J., Stewart-Brown, S., Sandercock, J. *et al.* (2005) 'The effectiveness and cost-effectiveness of parent training/ education programmes for the treatment of conduct disorder, including oppositional defiant disorder, in children.' *Health Technology Assessment 9*, 50.

DSS Research (2005) 'Research toolkit.' Online at www.dssresearch.com/toolkit/sscalc/size.asp (accessed 5 May 2006).

HMSO (2003) *Every Child Matters.* Cm5860. London: HMSO.

Leve, L. and Chamberlain, P. (2005) 'Association with delinquent peers: intervention effects for youth in the juvenile justice system.' *Journal of Abnormal Child Psychology 33*, 3, 339–47.

Parker, R. (1999) *Adoption Now: Messages from Research.* Chichester: John Wiley & Sons.

PSSRU (annual) *The Unit Costs of Health and Social Care.* Canterbury: Personal Social Services Research Unit. Online at www.pssru.ac.uk/publications (accessed 5 May 2006).

Quinton, D. (2004) *Supporting Parents: Messages from Research.* London: Jessica Kingsley Publishers.

Seebohm, F. (1968) *Report by the Committee on Local Authority and Allied Social Services.* Cmnd3703. London: HMSO.

Sinclair, I. (2005) *Fostering Now: Messages from Research.* London: Jessica Kingsley Publishers.

Thoburn, T., Chand, A. and Procter, J. (2005) *Child Welfare Services for Minority Ethnic Families: The Research Reviewed.* London: Jessica Kingsley Publishers.

Trowel, J., Kolvin, I., Weeramanthri, T., Sadowski, H., Berelowitz, M., Glasser, D. and Leitch, I. (2002) 'Psychotherapy for sexually abused girls: psychopathological outcome findings and patterns of change.' *British Journal of Psychiatry 180*, 234–47.

Selected reading on parenting programmes

Barlow, J., Parsons J. and Stewart-Brown, S. (2005) 'Preventing emotional and behavioural problems: the effectiveness of parenting programmes with children less than 3 years of age.' *Child Care Health Development 1*, 33–42.

Becker, S. with Lawrie, S. (2004) 'An A–Z of therapeutic approaches for pupils with challenging behaviour: A review of the research evidence on "what works" in secondary schools.' In S. Becker (ed) *Improving Behaviour Through Therapeutic Approaches: Research into Practice in Nottingham City Learning Support Units.* Nottingham: Excellence in Cities.

Dodge, K.A. (2003) 'Preventing aggressive behaviour early in life: Comments on Webster-Stratton, Lochman, and Domitrovich and Greenberg.' In R.E. Tremblay, R.G. Barr and R. De V. Peters (eds) *Encyclopedia on Early Childhood Development.* Montreal, Quebec: Centre of Excellence for Early Childhood Development. Online at: www.excellence-earlychildhood.ca/documents/DodgeANGxp.pdf (accessed 5 May 2006).

Kendrick, D., Elkan, R., Hewitt, M., Dewey, M., Blair, M., Robinson, J. *et al.* (2000) 'Does home visiting improve parenting and the quality of the home environment? A systematic review and meta-analysis.' *Archives of Disease in Childhood 82*, 443–51.

MacMillan, H.L., Thomas. B.H., Jamieson, E., Walsh, C.A., Boyle, M.H., Shannon, H.S. and Gafni, A. (2005) 'Effectiveness of home visitation by public-health nurses in prevention of the recurrence of child physical abuse and neglect: a randomised controlled trial.' *Lancet 365*, 9473, 1786–93.

Olds, D., Henderson, C.R. Jr, Cole, R., Eckenrode, J., Kitzman, H., Luckey, D., Pettit, L., Sidora, K., Morris, P. and Powers, J. (1998) 'Long-term effects of nurse home visitation on children's criminal and antisocial behavior: 15-year follow-up of a randomized controlled trial.' *Journal of the American Medical Association 280*, 14, 1238–44.

Romeo, R., Byford, S. and Knapp, M. (2005) 'Economic evaluations of child and adolescent mental health interventions: a systematic review.' *Journal of Child Psychology and Psychiatry 46*, 9, 919–30.

Webster-Stratton, C. (2003) *'Aggression in young children perspective: services proven to be effective in reducing aggression.'* Online at www.incredibleyears.com (accessed 5 May 2006).

Subject Index

Author Index

For enquiries or renewal at
Quarles LRC
Tel: 01708 455011 – Extension 4009